Busting the Bocage: American Combined Arms Operations in France, 6 June—31 July 1944

I0140140

by
Captain Michael D. Doubler

U.S. Army Command and General Staff College
Fort Leavenworth, Kansas 66027-6900

COMBAT STUDIES INSTITUTE

Library of Congress Cataloging-in Publication Data

Doubler, Michael D. (Michael Dale), 1955-
   Busting the Bocage.

Bibliography: p.
   1. World War, 1939-1945—Campaigns—France—Bocage normand.
   2. Bocage normand (France)—History.
   I. Title.
   D756.5.N6D68   1988   940.54'21   88-23757

CONTENTS

ILLUSTRATIONS

Figures

Maps

I. NORMANDY: THE CONTEXT
OF THE BATTLE

Introduction

Over forty years have passed since Allied armies landed in Normandy with the purpose of liberating western Europe and destroying Hitler's Third Reich. Despite this passage of time and extensive writings on the landings in France, officers and historians are still intensely interested in D-Day and the Normandy campaign. Indeed, a great deal remains to be learned about the U.S. Army's participation in the Normandy campaign, and a detailed examination of the fighting yields a fruitful case study for America's professional officer corps concerning how American soldiers performed in combat, how squads and platoons closed with and destroyed the enemy, and how the Army adapted methods to overcome a whole host of problems that it encountered in combat.

The broad conceptual framework for this study of the U.S. Army's efforts in France in 1944 originated with an idea borrowed from the eminent British military historian Michael Howard. In a speech to the Royal United Services Institute in October 1973, Howard examined the difficulties military establishments encounter in creating doctrine for the employment of their combat forces. Unlike other professionals, military leaders have no sure method of testing or verifying their doctrines and practices short of combat. Due to this drawback, Howard thought that peacetime military doctrine is usually faulty. Such weaknesses in doctrine, however, are not irresoluble. Once in combat, the military can recognize flaws in its doctrine and combat techniques and remedy them as quickly as possible. Ultimately, the advantage will go to the army that learns quickly from its mistakes and adapts promptly to a new and unfamiliar environment.[1]

This study attempts to identify the problems that hampered the operations of the U.S. First Army during the weeks immediately following the D-Day landings. In Normandy, inexperienced American combat units struggled with veteran German defenders on terrain specially suited for the defense. The U.S. Army was faced with the problem of conducting offensive operations in the Normandy hedgerow country—known as the Bocage. Shortcomings in preinvasion training and preparation resulted initially in uncoordinated efforts whenever American infantry, tanks, and artillery tried to combine forces during attacks. Technical deficiencies also hampered efforts.

1

More important, this study shows the processes by which the Army identified and overcame its problems. Through flexibility and determination in battle, coupled with ingenuity and innovativeness in the use of weaponry, the U.S. Army was able to push back a stubborn opponent and achieve victory. At all levels from squad leader to commanding general, the U.S. First Army sought to turn a bad situation to its advantage. Locked in combat with a formidable foe, American leaders relied on their previous training and experience, common sense, and knowledge of the capabilities of their equipment to forge together the uncoordinated, separate elements of the Army's combat arms into a unified, combined arms team.

The American experience in Normandy supports Michael Howard's assertion that the ability of armies to adapt in combat is a key ingredient in their success. In the seven weeks between D-Day and 31 July 1944, despite shortcomings in combat experience and the difficult Normandy terrain, the U.S. First Army defeated the Germans in a series of battles that placed a premium on leadership and ingenuity at the small-unit level. New tactics and technical innovations allowed First Army units to close with and destroy a well-prepared defender. By early August, the Americans had restored mobility to the battlefield, and the Allies began to push the Germans back in operations designed to carry the Allied armies to Paris and beyond.

U.S. Army Organization and Doctrine

On 6 June 1944, Allied forces landed on the European continent with the mission of occupying Nazi Germany and destroying its armed forces. By the end of June, Allied commanders realized that original estimates for their rate of advance into the interior of France were overly optimistic. In the British sector, units under the overall command of General Sir Bernard L. Montgomery were stalled in front of Caen, which had been a D-Day objective. Likewise, the Americans of the U.S. First Army, commanded by Lieutenant General Omar N. Bradley, found themselves behind schedule and engaged in a grueling war of attrition with the Germans on terrain specially suited for the defense.

Sallying forth from the D-Day beachheads, the American Army had plunged into Normandy hoping to destroy the German units that lay in its path. First Army soon found itself in very inhospitable terrain facing a determined and capable enemy. Slow progress and prohibitive losses made it clear that normal methods of attacks were unworkable. German positions could not be outflanked or turned, so the only recourse was to plunge directly into the face of their defenses. But before the U.S. Army took the risk of shattering itself on the Germans' positions, soldiers of all ranks speculated on how to best rupture the enemy's defenses.

The principal assets that American combat leaders in Normandy had to rely on to defeat the Germans were the firepower and capabilities of their equipment and their knowledge of tactical doctrine. They also wielded the combat formations of the U.S. Army that had been equipped and organized with the outbreak of war. A familiarity with the composition and capabilities of these combat units is essential in understanding the small-unit actions that took place in Normandy. A knowledge of Army doctrine also facilitates a better comprehension of the operations that commanders designed and expected their units to execute.

In 1940, the Army adopted a new divisional organization on the premise that infantry divisions should be simple, mobile, and trimmed of all nonessential troops and equipment. Called the "triangular" division because of its use of three infantry regiments as the basis of the division, the new division became the Army's workhorse during World War II. The triangular division was meant to be lean, agile, and optimally suited for the attack. The new organization became the blueprint for Regular Army infantry divisions, and National Guard divisions adopted the new structure after America's entry into the war.[2]

The basic composition of the triangular division was three infantry regiments and a variety of combat and combat support troops at the division level (see figure 1). Taken together, the weaponry within a triangular division gave commanders at all levels vast amounts of firepower. The division artillery was foremost in combat power among the assets found at division level. The division artillery had four battalions—three 105-mm howitzer battalions with twelve guns each and a 155-mm howitzer battalion with twelve guns. The standard infantry regiment, the next major command below division level, consisted of three infantry battalions, an antitank company, a cannon company, a headquarters company, a service company, and a medical detachment. The next lower organization was the infantry battalion. Three rifle companies, a heavy weapons company, and a headquarters company comprised an 871-man battalion. The rifle company consisted of 3 rifle platoons, a weapons platoon, and a small headquarters section and had a total manpower strength of 6 officers and 187 enlisted men. The weapons platoon was armed with two .30-caliber and one .50-caliber machine guns, three 60-mm mortars, and three 2.36-inch bazookas. Three infantry squads comprised a rifle platoon. Each rifle squad consisted of twelve men armed with ten M1 Garand rifles, one Browning automatic rifle, and one M1903 bolt-action Springfield rifle. Despite the awesome, aggregate firepower of the weapons within a triangular division, the lifeblood of the infantry division was the 5,211 officers and combat infantrymen who manned its 27 rifle companies.[3]

Ironically, in emphasizing the leanness and toughness of the triangular division, Army planners denied the division the organic support of the weapon that would prove so important in ground combat in World War II—the tank. Despite the impressive array of weaponry within the triangular infantry division, the firepower and mobility of tanks was a necessary augmentation to the infantry division's combat power. The need for effective combined arms operations was one of the principal tactical lessons of World War I and had been reaffirmed by the *Wehrmacht*'s victories early in World War II. For this reason, Army planners had not neglected tanks, neither in their role nor in their organizational composition.

At the outbreak of World War II, American armor had two combat roles, infantry support and exploitation. With the founding of the Armored Forces in July 1940, the groundwork was laid for the creation of the American armored division. The intended, primary role of the armored division was offensive operations against hostile rear areas. By 1943, the combat power of the armored division was based on an equal number of tanks, infantry, and artillery battalions within the division. Thus, the armored division, unlike its counterpart the triangular infantry division, was a true combined arms unit.[4]

The Army realized, however, that the triangular division needed armored support. Adamant in preserving the lightness of the triangular division, Army planners refused to incorporate a tank battalion into the standard organization of the infantry division. Instead, independent tank battalions were formed and became known as general headquarters (GHQ) tank units. The theory ran that GHQ tank battalions could be attached singly or in groups to infantry divisions for specific operations or that commanders at the highest levels could mass GHQ tank units for exploitation missions in much the same way as an armored division might be employed.[5]

Officers—761
Warrant officers—44
Enlisted men—13,238
TOTAL—14,043

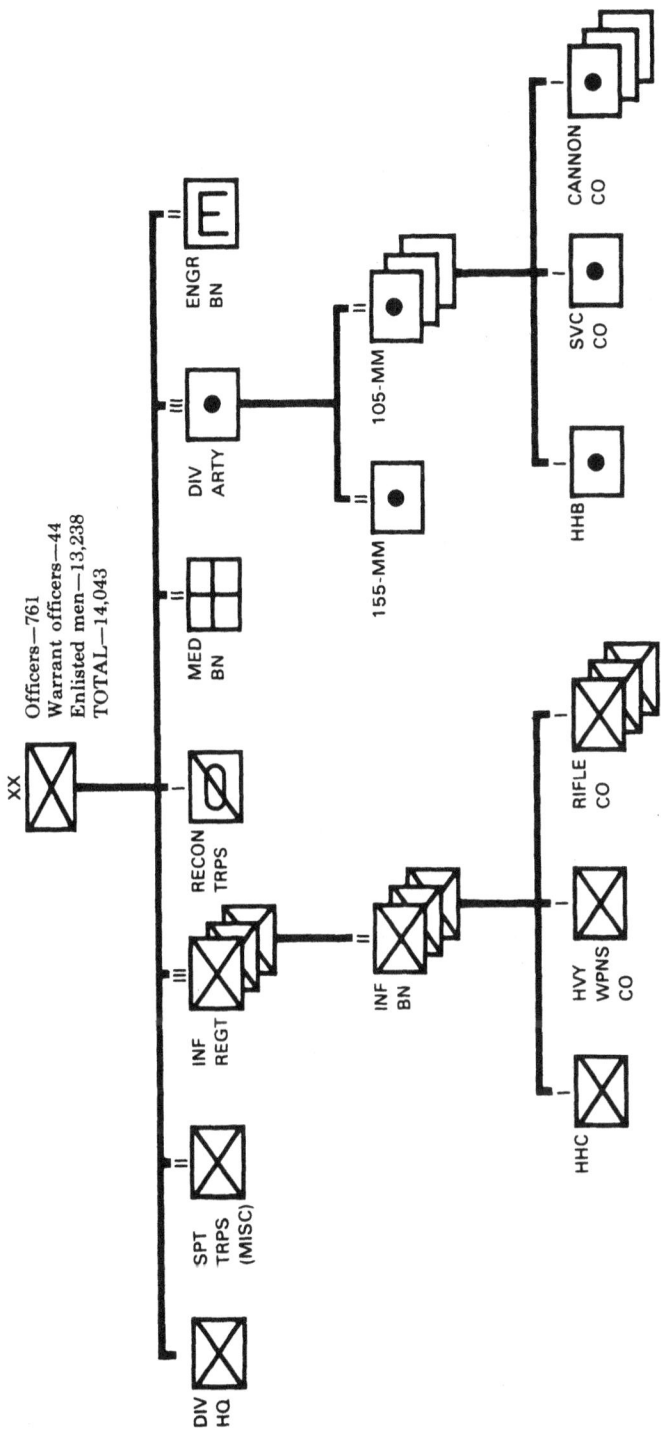

Adapted from *Evolution of the U.S. Army Division, 1939–1968* (Fort Belvoir, VA: Combat Operations Research Group: Headquarters, U.S. Combat Developments Command, 1969), p. 48.

Figure 1. Triangular infantry division (1943)

Regardless of whether a tank battalion served in an armored division or as a GHQ tank unit, the organization was the same. A standard tank battalion consisted of a headquarters company, a service company, three medium tank companies, and a light tank company. Each tank platoon had five tanks—two tanks in a "light" section and three tanks in a "heavy" section. Every tank company had three platoons and a headquarters section of two tanks. The medium tank company had a total strength of 5 officers and 116 enlisted men and was equipped with 17 M-4 Sherman tanks. The light tank company had five officers and ninety-one enlisted men and was equipped with the M-5 Stuart light tank.[6]

Single GHQ tank battalions were normally assigned to infantry divisions to provide support during operations. In turn, the tank battalion was attached to one of the division's infantry regiments and then operated closely with the battalions of that regiment. In an infantry division, the separate elements of the combined arms team came together at the regimental level. A GHQ tank unit, detachments from the division's engineer battalion, fire-support elements from the division artillery and supporting combat aviation, and the rifle battalions of the infantry regiment were the active participants in the combined arms team of World War II. Supporting elements were often not held at the regimental level but were passed on to the rifle battalions. A single rifle battalion in the attack might be augmented by tanks, combat engineers, artillery support, and the firepower of fighter-bombers.

American military leaders in Normandy were familiar with the body of knowledge that was the basis for the American methods of waging war. Field Manual (FM) 100-5, *Field Service Regulations, Operations*, served as the conceptual foundation for the Army's ideas on battle doctrine that were conceived and implemented prior to and during World War II. The manual described the fundamental doctrines of combat operations, the basic concepts of battlefield leadership, and the principles of employment for the combat arms. Additionally, FM 100-5 spread its influence over the Army's school system and formed the common link between all training and instruction carried out at the various service schools.

The military subject matter covered by the 1941 edition of FM 100-5 was broad and diverse. However, two root concepts occur again and again throughout the discussions on the roles of the combat arms and the conduct of military operations. The first was the critical importance of dynamic, competent leadership. Commanding troops in combat was a complex task that required leaders to possess "will power, self confidence, initiative, and disregard of self," as well as superior knowledge about technical and tactical matters. In the introduction to FM 100-5, Army Chief of Staff General George C. Marshall stressed that it was a function of competent leadership to combine doctrinal concepts with battlefield experience to produce plans that would ensure success in battle.[7]

Ironically, the coordination of the combat arms, which was deficient in the beginning phases of the Normandy battles, was the second theme that ran throughout FM 100-5. Officers of the expanding, modernizing U.S. Army of the early 1940s were aware of the importance of coordinated, concerted action by the combat arms. FM 100-5 stated that "no one arm wins battles." The "combined action of all arms and services" was the key to success. Unit commanders were held responsible for coordinating the "tactics and techniques of the various arms" and for developing in their units the combined arms teamwork "essential to success."[8]

A better comprehension of the Army's offensive doctrine contained in FM 100-5 enhances an understanding of First Army's struggle in Normandy. According to FM 100-5, the sole purpose of offensive operations was the destruction of hostile armed forces. To achieve this purpose, a commander established a clearly defined physical objective toward which all efforts could be directed. Attacks were grouped into two categories: envelopments and penetrations. Of these two forms of attack, the envelopment was the more preferable. The design for an attack consisted of a plan of maneuver and a plan of fire. FM 100-5 stated that the best guarantee for success in an attack was the effective cooperation between the troops in the attacking echelon, the supporting artillery, and any supporting combat aviation. The "superior commander" was that battle leader who could coordinate his fire support with his plan of maneuver.[9]

From the doctrinal framework provided by FM 100-5, the Army's various combat arms, working under the supervision of the War Department, generated more detailed offensive doctrines for their respective arms. The techniques and procedures developed by the combat arms specifically described how each arm would perform in battle and interact with other combat arms during operations. In turn, these doctrines served as the basis for combat training conducted in the Army's service schools and maneuver units.

The Army's primary ground-gaining arm was the infantry. Because of its ability to seize or retain major objectives, the infantry battalion was the most basic combat unit of the U.S. Army. Infantry doctrine prescribed that battalions usually attacked in daylight to seize terrain objectives. While envelopments were preferred over penetrations, infantry doctrine admitted that the battalion-size attacks were usually nothing more than frontal assaults against enemy defenses. Battalions attacked along a frontage of 500—1,000 yards in width, depending on terrain and enemy dispositions. The rifle companies of the infantry battalion performed the actual tasks of seizing objectives and closing with the enemy. Normally, a battalion attacked with two companies abreast, the third company acting as the battalion reserve. One of the attacking companies conducted the main attack, while the other supported the main effort with secondary attacks. A single rifle company's zone of attack was usually 200—500 yards wide.[10]

Army doctrine recognized that the infantry was capable of only "limited independent action" through the employment of its organic weapons. The other combat arms had to augment the infantry to increase its offensive power to overcome strong enemy defenses. Recognizing the infantry's need, each of the Army's combat arms developed doctrine in support of the infantry's attacks.[11]

FM 17-36 outlined the techniques used by armored forces when operating in conjunction with the infantry. Like FM 100-5, this manual stressed the need for closer cooperation and coordination between the ground forces. FM 17-36 insisted that since the role of tanks and infantry "are linked so closely" that it was essential that the "doctrine, powers and limitations of both" be understood by those involved.[12]

Tanks operating with infantry during offensive operations assisted the infantry by destroying the enemy with firepower and by keeping the attack moving using the tanks' inherent armored protection and mobility. The combat capabilities of tanks and infantry were complementary. Prewar doctrine specified that infantry-armor attack formations consisted of two separate echelons. Armor led when the terrain was suitable and when antitank weapons and obstacles were absent or neutralized. Infantry led the attack over difficult terrain and when strong enemy minefields and antitank defenses were present. When armor led the attack, the first attacking echelon was composed solely of tanks, while the second echelon comprised infantry and tanks. Similarly, if infantry led the attack, the first wave was composed solely of infantry formations, while the second wave comprised tank-infantry teams. Despite the firepower produced by small arms, machine guns, and tank main guns in tank-infantry forces, tactical doctrine acknowledged that this firepower in no way minimized the need for close support from the other combat arms.[13]

Foremost among the support provided by the other combat arms was the firepower of the field artillery. Commanders fully integrated supporting fires into the attack so that they would coincide with the time of attack and the scheme of maneuver. Artillery's role in the combined arms attack was to neutralize enemy crew-served weapons, to destroy field fortifications, and to prevent enemy infantry from manning their defenses as the U.S. assault approached its objective. When the tank-infantry forces were prepared to conduct the final assault, artillery fires were lifted upon request and then shifted onto other enemy targets beyond the objective.[14]

Combat engineers formed another important adjunct to the tank-infantry team. Engineers had the overall mission of increasing combat effectiveness through acts of construction or demolition designed to facilitate friendly movement or to hinder the enemy's mobility. When operating with tank-infantry forces in offensive operations, engineers usually had a mobility enhancement mission, which meant they were to remove or breach obstacles such as antitank ditches, wire entanglements, and minefields.[15]

Combat Experience Before D-Day

Knowledge of Army doctrine and weaponry were not the only assets available to First Army leaders seeking to find new ways to win in the Bocage. Lessons learned during combat operations prior to D-Day helped provide some basis for developing solutions to problems encountered in Normandy. Combat experience among American commanders and their troops in France varied greatly. Unblooded units whose only firsthand knowledge of military operations was training maneuvers in the United States and England joined divisions that had fought in North Africa and Sicily. While only some American troops had actually been in combat, most were aware of the major combat lessons learned in the North African and Mediterranean theaters.

Despite successes in Tunisia and Sicily, the U.S. Army that assaulted the Normandy beaches was still far from being a well-oiled, coordinated fighting machine. Shortcomings in pre-battle training and battlefield coordination during 1942 and 1943 prevented the U.S. Army from developing its full potential as an effective fighting force. One of the major problems discovered was the surprising lack of aggressiveness displayed by infantry units. Instead of employing techniques of fire and maneuver to close with and destroy the enemy, infantry attacks often merely located and pinned down the enemy. Artillery fire was then called on to finish the infantry's job of destroying the defenders. Instead of relying on their organic weapons, infantrymen trusted in the big guns of the field artillery to deliver the coups de grace.[16]

Another problem compounded the infantry's reliance on artillery support. The purpose of the infantry division's mortars and assault guns was to support the attacks of the riflemen. Consequently, these weapons were usually employed close to the fighting front and became favorite targets for German artillery, tanks, and other heavy weapons. American mortar, antitank, and assault-gun crews often suffered heavy casualties. A tendency developed in which these weapons remained hidden and silent until the salvos of the supporting artillery landed on the defenders' positions. Artillery fires suppressed and neutralized the Germans, and only then would the infantry's organic heavy weapons join in the battle.[17]

Even more disturbing was the poor coordination that existed during tank-infantry attacks. Experience in combat painfully showed that stateside training lacked emphasis on the planning and execution of combined arms attacks. Infantry commanders habitually failed to exploit the mobility and firepower of the tanks attached to their units. Conversely, tankers operating with infantry were often reluctant to aggressively advance, taking the burden of the attack away from the riflemen. When the tankers did lead the attack, infantrymen had a tendency to lag behind and were slow in following the tanks to the objective. Tankers often found themselves in the predicament of being on their objectives and surrounded by pockets of German defenders while still awaiting the arrival of their accompanying infantry. On the other hand, riflemen who stayed with their tanks during the attack were often killed or wounded by stray enemy fire from heavy weaponry intended for the American tanks. Inadequate communications at the lowest levels also hampered smoothly executed tank-infantry attacks. Often infantry platoons could not warn the tankers about antitank traps and weapons.

Answers to the perplexing problems of tank-infantry coordination were still lacking prior to the Normandy battles.[18]

Battles in the Mediterranean and North African theaters exposed numerous organizational weaknesses in the Army. Perhaps the most significant was the existence of separate, independent GHQ tank battalions. These units, considered inferior in maintenance and training to their counterparts in armored divisions, were usually quickly rotated between different infantry units, not only within a single division but among other divisions as well. At the small-unit level, this made the development of the teamwork and esprit so important to the success of the tank-infantry team almost impossible. Because of their independent existence, GHQ tank battalions lacked proper care and support. Outside of a regular division's personnel and supply channels, GHQ tank battalions suffered from lack of crew replacements, supplies, and spare parts. Unfortunately, GHQ tank battalions were often indifferently commanded, the best armor officers being chosen to command tank battalions within armored divisions. The problem of GHQ tank battalions was a sore one and accompanied the U.S. Army to the French mainland.[19]

The Operational Setting

Within a few days after the Allied invasion of Normandy, the U.S. Army found itself facing a stubborn opponent on terrain that favored the defender. Units fought desperately for hills, towns, and bridges that had become of strategic importance. At every turn, the Americans faced the seasoned veterans of the German Army. The effects of weather and especially terrain had a direct influence on the conduct of operations, while the dispositions and defensive capabilities of the German Army crucially dictated American actions. A familiarity with these factors is essential to a full understanding of the Normandy campaign (see map 1).

The terrain features of the French countryside had a particularly strong influence on the conduct of operations. The terrain on the Allied left, held by the British Second Army, was an expanse of gently rolling pastures and cultivated fields. The relatively dry and firm ground in the British sector facilitated armor operations and the construction of forward airfields. The boundary line between the British Second Army and the U.S. First Army began on the coast near Port-en-Bessin and extended

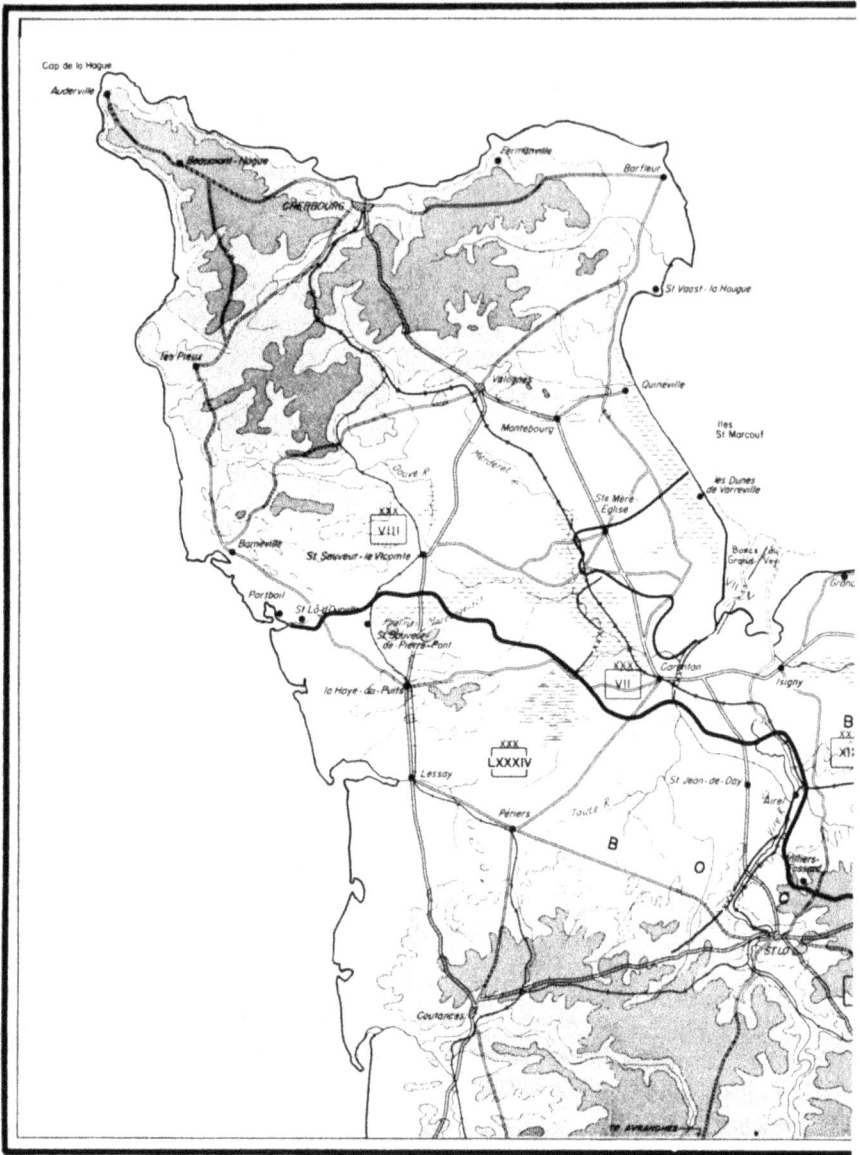

Map 1. The advance inland, 6 June—1 July 1944

inland for approximately twenty miles, ending a few miles east of the village of Caumont. The U.S. First Army was responsible for operations along a wide arc that stretched westward from Caumont to the port of Cherbourg, a frontage of more than fifty miles.[20]

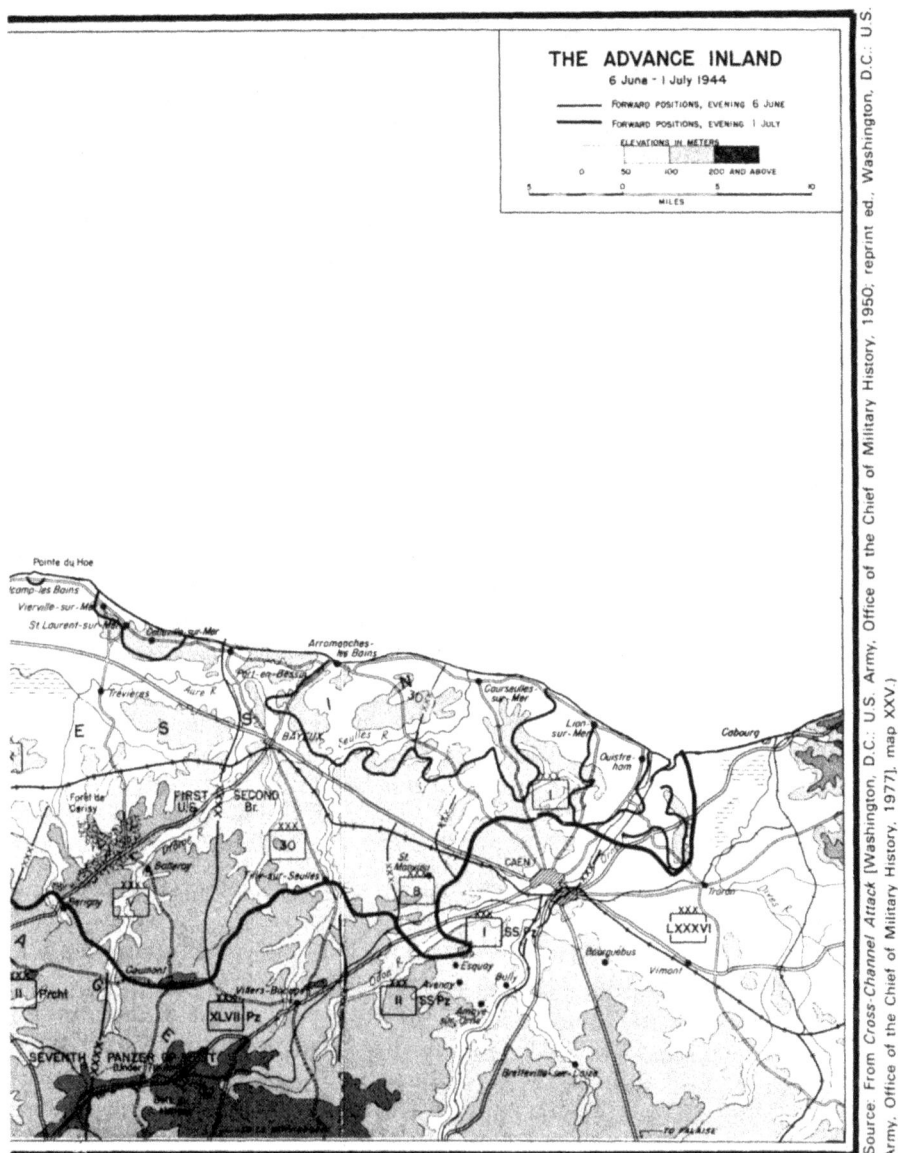

THE ADVANCE INLAND
6 June - 1 July 1944

FORWARD POSITIONS, EVENING 6 JUNE
FORWARD POSITIONS, EVENING 1 JULY

ELEVATIONS IN METERS

0   50   100   200 AND ABOVE

MILES

Unlike the terrain in the British sector, the ground held by the U.S. First Army did not favor mobile operations. The American left, the ground between the boundary line with the British and the Vire River, was broken and uneven. The countryside in this sector was a patchwork of small hills, low ridges, narrow rivers, and steep valleys that hampered long-range observation and impeded cross-country movement. The center of the American sector was low ground that contained extensive marshlands. The whole area was drained by the Taute and Vire Rivers, which empty into the English Channel near Carentan and Isigny, respectively. The marshlands are flat, and the ground is soft and moist making travel by foot difficult, with vehicle traffic being almost impossible. Heavy rains make the marshlands even less trafficable, restricting movement to the few asphalt roads that traverse the bogs. On the American right, the terrain was more favorable. Between the marshes in the center of the sector and the coastline on the extreme right flank, a group of hills rose up to dominate the northern end of the Cotentin Peninsula. The most important terrain feature on the American right was the city of Cherbourg with its extensive port facilities.

Several miles inland, the low terrain throughout the First Army sector rose into a plateau with average heights of 200 meters above sea level. The plateau started along the line Coutances—Saint-Lô—Bayeux and stretched southward into the French interior. As American units advanced inland, they would have to conduct attacks to dislodge German units from the high terrain features on the rim of the plateau. Some of the most bitter fighting of the Normandy campaign took place around Saint-Lô, as American units pushed back German troops entrenched on the high ground around the village.

The compartmentalized nature of the countryside was the most striking feature of the terrain in the U.S. First Army sector. The swamplands restricted all cross-country maneuver, making the use and control of the road network a necessity for offensive operations. The natural, uneven lay of the land in the rest of the American sector made command and control of deployed combat forces extremely difficult. Despite these natural obstacles, the most pervasive and formidable barrier in the American sector was man-made.

For centuries, Norman farmers had followed the practice of enclosing the plots of their arable land, pastures as well as orchards, with thick hedgerows. The hedgerow country in the U.S. sector started about ten miles inland from the Normandy beaches and extended in a wide swath from Caumont on the American left to the western coast of the Cotentin Peninsula. The hedgerows are sturdy embankments, half earth, half hedge. At their base, they resemble dirt parapets and vary in thickness from one to four feet, with heights that range from three to fifteen feet. Growing out of this earthen wall is a hedge that consists of small trees and tangles of vines and brush. This vegetation has a thickness of between one to three feet and varies in height from three to fifteen feet. Originally intended to serve as fences to mark land boundaries, to keep in livestock, and to prevent the erosion of the the land by sea winds, the hedgerows surround each field, breaking the terrain into numerous walled enclosures. Because the fields are small, about 200 by 400 yards in size, and usually irregular in shape, the hedgerows are numerous and set in no logical pattern. Each field has an opening in the hedgerow that permits access for humans, livestock, and farm equipment. For passage to fields that are not adjacent to regular highways, numerous wagon trails run through the hedgerows.

The military features of the Bocage are obvious. The hedgerows divide the country into tiny compartments. The hedgerows in each field provide excellent cover and concealment to the defender and present a formidable obstacle to the attacker. Numerous adjoining fields can be organized to form a natural defensive position echeloned in depth. The thick vegetation provides excellent camouflage and limits the deployment of units. The hedgerows also restrict observation, making the effective use of heavy-caliber direct-fire weapons almost impossible and hampering the adjustment of artillery fire. Anyone occupying a high place that afforded good fields of observation and a clear view of the surrounding countryside would have a distinct advantage.

The uneven and compartmentalized nature of the Bocage put increased emphasis on the importance of the network of paved roads in the First Army sector. The main highways either paralleled the coast or stretched inland to the interior of Normandy. Carentan, in the center of the First Army's sector, was a vital road junction. From this village, good highways ran eastward to Périers and La Haye-du-Puits. East of Carentan, two parallel roads ran south to Saint-Lô, which was perhaps the most vital road junction in the First Army sector. Like spokes on a wheel, roads ran from Saint-Lô in almost every direction. The force that could hold Saint-Lô would retain control over much of the road network in the Bocage.

Like the terrain, the weather also influenced operations in Normandy. More than anything else, persistent rains during June and July hampered the efforts of the U.S. Army. The early summer of 1944 was the wettest since 1900.[21] Extended periods of rainy weather turned the marshlands west of Carentan into

An aerial view of typical hedgerow terrain in Normandy. Note the irregular-shaped pattern of the fields.

a bottomless morass, making cross-country movement impossible. Rains also added immeasurably to the daily miseries endured by the foot soldier. Low visibility and cloud ceilings often grounded all aircraft, denying the ground forces the support of fighter-bombers and aerial observers that was so desperately needed. Additionally, a major channel storm ravaged the invasion beaches during 19—23 June, severely restricting the movement of supplies onto the mainland. As a result, shortages in key commodities hampered operations during the battles in the Bocage. The extent of daylight was also important. Extremely long days put a premium on the hours of darkness. Nighttime was used to rearm, resupply, rest, and plan for the next day's operations. Short nights limited the amount of time for these activities, and early dawns often found exhausted American units unprepared to conduct an attack or to defend against counterattacks.

Of all the factors that influenced Allied operations in the summer of 1944, none was more significant than the German Army's determination and defensive abilities. Since 6 June, German soldiers had fought desperately to contain the expanding Allied beachheads. Most were unaware of heated controversies taking place in the German High Command over the best way to repel the Allied invasion. The German commander in chief in western Europe, Field Marshal Gerd von Rundstedt, favored a mobile defense. Rundstedt disagreed with his most trusted subordinate, Field Marshal Erwin Rommel. The "Desert Fox" commanded Army Group B and bore direct responsibility for the defense of the northern coastlines of France. Rommel favored a strong forward defense that would defeat the Allied invasion on the beaches. Adolf Hitler was aware of the disagreement between his western commanders, but he failed to settle the dispute. Consequently, the Germans adopted neither the forward nor the mobile defense concepts as a distinct course of action.

After D-Day, Rundstedt and Rommel cooperated in concentrating forces to eliminate the Allied beachheads. They proposed to Hitler that the Germans fight a series of defensive battles while assembling forces for a massive counterattack. However, on 25 June, a major British attack near Caen forced the Germans to commit all of their reserves. The Germans now found themselves defending along a static line with few forces left to mount any large-scale counterattacks. Both Rundstedt and Rommel's previous operational concepts for the defense of Normandy were now irrelevant.

On 29 June, Hitler himself intervened and announced a new plan for the defense of France. The Führer believed that German forces had to prevent the Allies from gaining an opportunity to conduct mobile warfare in the west. Before they could conduct a blitz campaign, the Allies needed sufficient space to deploy their formations and favorable terrain on which to maneuver. Hitler believed the best way to prevent an Allied blitzkrieg was to contain the expansion of the British and American beachheads. Thus, the Führer ordered German forces to engage the Allies in a savage battle of static warfare along a strong line that would capitalize on the defensive characteristics of the Bocage. Hitler knew his units occupied extremely favorable defensive positions, so he ordered the German Army to stay and fight to the last in Normandy.

The German Seventh Army, under the command of General Paul Hausser, opposed the U.S. First Army. Seventh Army consisted of three fresh infantry divisions, the remnants of four more infantry divisions that had suffered heavy casualties during the early fighting in Normandy, a parachute regiment, and three regimental-size combat teams known in the German Army as *kampfgruppen*. These troops were organized into two corps, the LXXXIV Corps and the II Parachute Corps. The LXXXIV

Corps was responsible for operations west of the Vire River, while the II Parachute Corps defended the sector between Saint-Lô and Caumont. The aggregate strength of Seventh Army was 35,000 combat troops, with all of their organic weaponry supported by approximately 80 tanks.

In carrying out Hitler's orders for the stubborn defense of Normandy, General Hausser deployed his troops along a fixed front and intended to make the Americans fight and die for each inch of ground. The Germans lightly manned their forward defense line, keeping the bulk of their combat troops in reserve. These reserves were grouped into counterattack units and were supported by tanks and assault guns. Once the German forward lines identified the main American assault, reserves would counterattack the flanks and rear of the Americans. Well aware of the hedgerows that favored their defensive efforts, the Germans coined their tactics "bush warfare."

Compared with the German High Command, Allied leadership was in much wider agreement about the overall strategy for the invasion campaign. The Allied plan for the invasion of western Europe consisted of two phases. The first was the seizure and establishment of secure beachheads large enough to permit the landing of substantial combat forces with adequate supply levels. The second phase of the Allied strategy called for expanding the coastal enclaves into a substantial lodgment area. Such an area would provide for the deployment of enough combat forces, both ground and air along with support units and sufficient supplies, to ensure the success of a mass offensive into central France and toward Germany.

Landing in France on 6 June, the U.S. First Army under General Bradley quickly consolidated its foothold on the Normandy beaches. Elements of Major General J. Lawton Collins' VII Corps seized Utah Beach, while units of Major General Leonard T. Gerow's V Corps assaulted Omaha Beach. Moving to complete the first phase of Allied strategy by securing and expanding their beachheads, the U.S. V and VII Corps began to push inland. By 12 June, the Americans had captured Carentan and effected a linkup between the heretofore separate beachheads. Meanwhile, combat units of Major General Charles H. Corlett's XIX Corps arrived in France to reinforce the U.S. effort. [22]

Confident that First Army had sufficient forces in France to prevent the Germans from eliminating the beachheads, General Bradley moved to implement the second phase of

Allied strategy. On 14 June, VII Corps launched an offensive to seize the badly needed port facilities at Cherbourg. Collins' offensive enjoyed good success, and Cherbourg fell on 26 June. While Collins moved against Cherbourg, consuming the majority of available supplies, the remainder of First Army stood on the defensive warding off German attacks and preparing for future operations.[23]

By 1 July, with the American beachheads secure, First Army prepared to resume the offensive. The U.S. Army was deployed along a wide arc that stretched from Caumont to the west coast of the Cotentin Peninsula near La Haye-du-Puits. General Bradley's mission was to continue the expansion of the lodgment area and to relieve German pressure against the British by conducting a full offensive against the German Seventh Army. Scheduled for 1 July, the attack was designed to push the Germans out of Normandy and to open the way for American operations into Brittany.

For the attack, Bradley had available the equivalent of thirteen divisions organized into four separate corps. On the American right was Major General Troy H. Middleton's VIII Corps, consisting of the 82d Airborne and 79th and 90th Infantry Divisions. The newly arrived 8th Division was also assigned to VIII Corps to replace the 82d Airborne, which was scheduled to return to England for rest and refit. To the left of VIII Corps, in the vicinity of Carentan, was Collins' VII Corps. Three infantry divisions, the 83d, 4th, and 9th, were under VII Corps control. On Collins' left stood Corlett's XIX Corps, which consisted of the 29th, 30th, and 35th Infantry Divisions and newly arrived elements of the 3d Armored Division. Major General Gerow's V Corps held the American left flank and was anchored on the village of Caumont. The V Corps had under its command the 1st and 2d Infantry Divisions and the 2d Armored Division. Out of the total number of divisions in Normandy, less than half (the 1st, 2d, 4th, and 9th Infantry Divisions, the 82d Airborne, and the 2d Armored) had any combat experience. For the other units in First Army, their initial experience in combat would be among the Normandy hedgerows.[24]

II. THE BATTLE
Tactical Problems

By early July, First Army was painfully aware of its slow progress, as it fell far behind preinvasion estimates of advance. Planners within Supreme Headquarters, Allied Expeditionary Force (SHAEF), thought that by 20 June (D+14) First Army would be far inland occupying the line Lessay—Saint-Lô—Caumont. But not for another month would First Army occupy the entire area within the D+14 sector. American commanders said their progress was slowed by the inhospitable hedgerow country, the tenacity and organization of the German defense, and various inadequacies within the American combined arms team.[1]

The formidable barriers presented by the hedgerows and the military characteristics of the Bocage seem to have taken First Army by complete surprise. Despite Allied planners' awareness of the nature of the Bocage, American commanders had done little to prepare their units for fighting among the hedgerows. Preoccupied with the myriad problems of the D-Day landings, American leaders had failed to see the battlefield in depth and had paid little attention to the potential problems of hedgerow combat. As early as 8 June, General Bradley called the Bocage the "damndest country I've seen." General Collins of VII Corps was equally surprised by the nature of the hedgerow terrain and told General Bradley on 9 June that the Bocage was as bad as anything he had encountered on Guadalcanal. Brigadier General James M. Gavin, the assistant division commander of the 82d Airborne, best summarized the surprise of the senior American leadership: "Although there had been some talk in the U.K. before D-Day about the hedgerows, none of us had really appreciated how difficult they would turn out to be."[2]

The junior leadership within First Army shared their seniors' surprise. In a survey conducted after the Normandy battles, not 1 out of 100 officers questioned stated that they had prior knowledge of the nature of the hedgerows. A summary of these interviews stated that the officers as a whole were "greatly surprised" by the Bocage. Captain Charles D. Folsom, a company commander in the 329th Infantry of VII Corps' 83d Infantry Division, admitted that the hedgerows presented a problem his unit "had never before encountered" and that preinvasion training had "not taken the hedgerows into consideration."[3]

An American fighting position in the Bocage. Note the heavy vegetation.

Courtesy Dwight D. Eisenhower Library

Even though the hedgerows were serious impediments to offensive operations, the primary obstacle holding up the American advance was the German defense. As First Army fought its way inland, it discovered that the German Army was well prepared and adept at defending the hedgerow country. The German defense was organized in depth and designed to destroy the coordination and momentum of American attacks while exploiting the defensive advantages of the hedgerows. The forward German defensive line was a series of interconnected, compartmentalized fields. Small detachments defended each field and its surrounding hedgerows. Behind these forward positions, the Germans organized a defensive zone consisting of echeloned belts of prepared battle positions. Available tanks and assault guns were distributed throughout the battle zone to blunt American attacks and to support German counterattacks.[4]

In addition, the Germans organized each field as a defensive strongpoint and confronted the attacking Americans with a deadly mixture of direct and indirect fires (see figure 2). The Germans employed their direct-fire weapons to trap American infantrymen in a deadly hail of cross fire and grazing fires coming from all sides. Machine guns were the primary weapons of the German defense. At the opposite corners of each field, the Germans emplaced heavy machine guns in positions dug into the earthen embankments of the hedgerows. The purpose of the heavy machine guns was to pin down attacking infantrymen in the open, making them easy targets for small arms and preplanned indirect fires. Light machine guns and machine pistols supplemented the fire of the heavy machine guns and were emplaced in other firing positions to the front and flanks of the attackers. The Germans also used their light machine guns to place bands of grazing fire along the bases of hedgerows paralleling the American attack. The purpose of the grazing fire was to inflict casualties on American infantrymen seeking cover and concealment during their advance. Indirect fire was a key component of the German defense. Once pinned down in the open, preplanned artillery and mortar fire punished American units. German mortar fire was particularly effective, causing as much as 75 percent of all U.S. casualties during the Normandy campaign.[5]

The Germans also implemented other measures to improve their scheme of hedgerow defenses. They habitually dug slit trenches into the hedgerow embankments to protect themselves during American artillery and mortar barrages. Furthermore, German commanders linked together their defensive positions with wire communications that allowed them to coordinate the defense of their sector. Snipers also were an important part of the German defense. They were used to protect machine-gun positions against infiltrating Americans and to deliver harassing fire during lulls in the action. Booby traps and mines abounded within the thick vegetation of the hedgerows. Trip-wire explosives were a German favorite. To combat American armor at close range, German infantry used the *panzerfaust* (a light, portable weapon, fired by one man, that launched an armor-piercing rocket). At longer ranges, Germans engaged American armor with tank main guns, self-propelled guns, and used the legendary 88-mm antiaircraft gun in a ground-defense mode.[6]

The early fighting in Normandy demonstrated the effectiveness of the German defensive system. American infantry commanders soon realized that normal tactical maneuvers were impossible in the Bocage. Company commanders initially used conventional methods of attack, with two rifle platoons abreast followed in turn by the third rifle platoon and the weapons platoon. However, companies could not deploy and maneuver because of thick vegetation and the compartmentalized nature

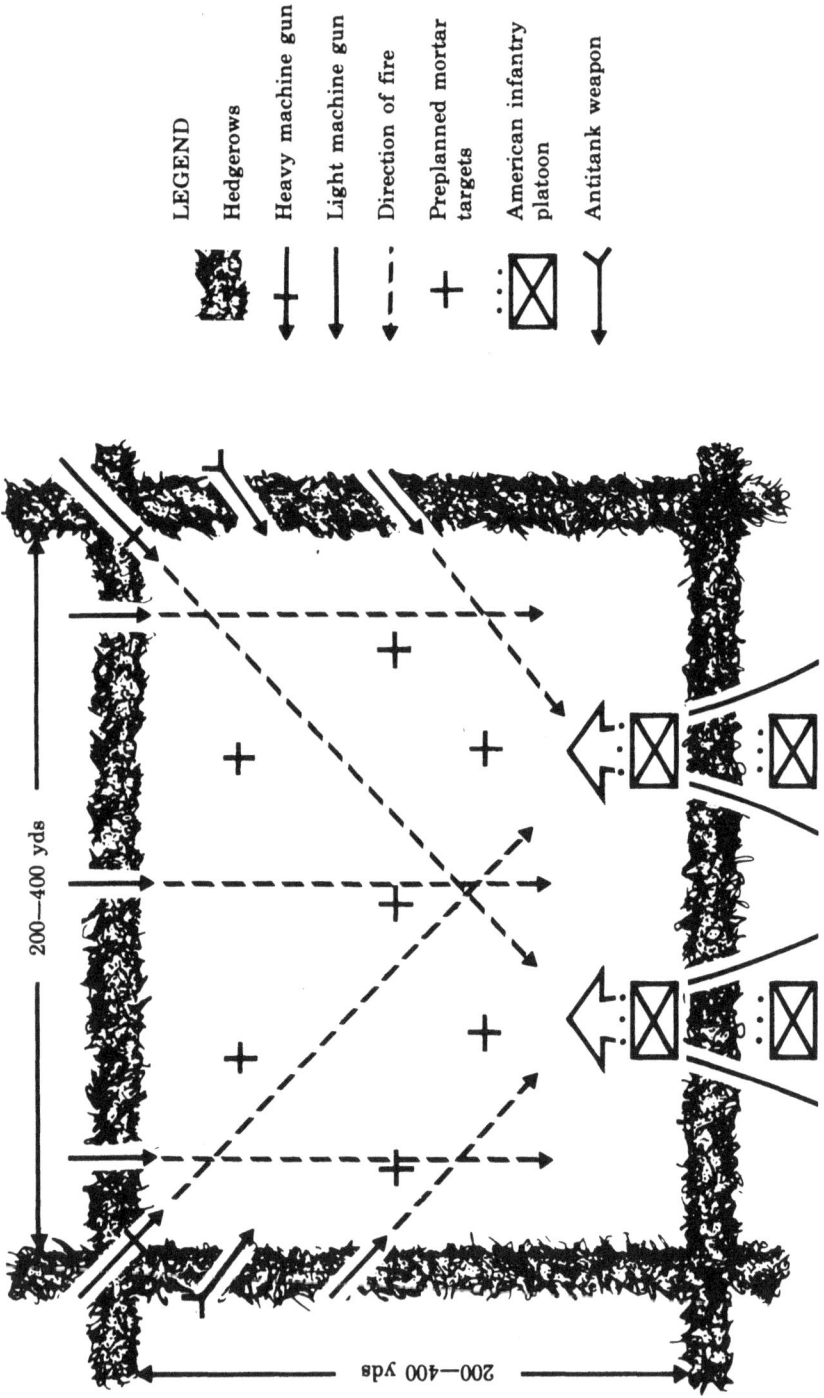

LEGEND

Hedgerows	
Heavy machine gun	
Light machine gun	
Direction of fire	
Preplanned mortar targets	
American infantry platoon	
Antitank weapon	

200—400 yds

200—400 yds

Figure 2. German hedgerow defense

of the terrain. Platoons were forced to hack their way through the dense vegetation because German defensive fires covered all natural breaks in the hedgerows. As leading attack elements emerged from the hedgerows, they found themselves exposed to almost point-blank German machine-gun fire. Pinned down in the open in the middle of a well-prepared kill zone, infantrymen were unable to maneuver and continue the attack. Squads returned fire with their own rifles and automatic weapons, but their firepower was not enough to suppress the defenders. American commanders quickly discovered that four or five German defensive positions could pin down an entire infantry battalion and hold up an attack for long periods.[7]

Unable to use normal techniques of fire and maneuver, American commanders were also powerless to influence the battle with increased firepower. Heavy vegetation and the close proximity of the German defenders made it impossible to bring forward and set up heavy machine guns. Company commanders used their organic 60-mm mortars in an attempt to knock out German machine-gun positions. However, the hedgerows and the close combat conditions made the observation and adjustment of mortar and artillery fire almost impossible. American and German units often fought one another at ranges of less than 300 yards. Short distances made calling for artillery fire risky, since unadjusted rounds could easily land on friendly troops. Many engagements were fought at such close range that even if friendly rounds landed on German positions, the effects of shrapnel and concussion would endanger American lives. Unable to observe the enemy and to call fire on him from a safe distance, infantrymen were deprived of field artillery and mortar support.[8]

The Bocage also adversely affected command and control of small units. Companies and battalions did not attack along fixed frontages as prescribed in standard doctrine. Instead of attacking along a frontage of between 200 and 500 yards, company-size attacks were canalized into single fields. Likewise, battalions attacked on fronts as narrow as 300 yards in order to seize a group of adjacent hedgerow fields. Standard control measures and boundary lines between units were almost meaningless in the compartmentalized terrain. Commanders learned to orient their attacks along roads and paths running through the Bocage. At the company level, maintaining proper orientation during an attack proved difficult. Hemmed in on all sides by the hedgerows, platoons lost their sense of direction and without a fixed reference point often became disoriented and could not pinpoint their own location on their maps. These orientation problems aggravated normal difficulties in getting platoons and companies to advance under fire.[9]

Bad terrain and the Germans' tactical proficiency were not the only conditions hampering operations. American commanders observed many defects in the training and effectiveness of their troops. As experience in other theaters had shown, lack of aggressiveness was a major problem in most infantry units. Infantrymen failed to maneuver in order to place more effective direct fire on the enemy. Instead, units maneuvered to locate the Germans and then called for heavy weapons and indirect fire to neutralize the defenders. Even after the artillery had pounded enemy positions, many infantry units were slow in seizing their objectives. General Bradley acknowledged that a major problem in First Army was the infantry's slowness in following their close supporting artillery barrages.[10]

Interrogation of German prisoners during the hedgerow battles revealed that even the Germans detected a lack of aggressive drive among the American infantry units. Prisoners stated that the American infantry moved too cautiously and consequently failed to take weakly held positions. They were surprised that artillery barrages were not followed up by determined infantry assaults. An experienced corporal in the German 275th Infantry Division summed up German attitudes: "Americans use infantry cautiously. If they used it the way Russians do, they would be in Paris now."[11]

American infantrymen were not convinced of the potency and effectiveness of their own rifle and machine-gun fires. Their failure to maintain the proper distribution and volume of small-arms fire during assaults was a major problem. Infantry training stressed covering the entire objective with small-arms fire during an attack to suppress enemy defensive fires. In Normandy, many riflemen failed to keep up a steady rate of fire during the attack. Instead, they tended not to fire at suspected enemy positions but to wait for a definite target before opening fire. Consequently, many concealed German positions were not fired on during the attack.[12]

Inexperience in combat also hampered infantry units. In battle for the first time, infantrymen had to rely on their training and leaders to get them through the initial trauma of combat. Many had to learn how to survive through their own experiences and from the misfortunes of others. Green troops of all ranks had a tendency not to move under fire, preferring the

Infantrymen crouching behind bushes atop a hedgerow

protection of the closest cover or simply hugging the open ground. German snipers were a particular source of fear.[13] The experience of a platoon leader in the 9th Division illustrates how untried troops can react under fire:

> One of the fatal mistakes made by infantry replacements is to hit the ground and freeze when fired upon. Once I ordered a squad to advance from one hedgerow to another. During the movement one man was shot by a sniper firing one round. The entire squad hit the ground and they were picked off, one by one, by the same sniper.[14]

For normal infantrymen, becoming "battle wise" was a terrible, if not fatal, experience.

Tankers also found the hedgerow country forbidding. They discovered that vegetation and the compartmentalized nature of the terrain negated their best assets, mobility and firepower. The hedgerows kept the tanks from maneuvering freely, and poor observation prevented the tankers from using their long-range main guns and machine guns. Tanks unaccompanied by friendly infantry were easy targets for German infantry armed with explosives and *panzerfausts*. Reluctant to operate within the confined spaces and tangles of the hedgerows, tank commanders kept their vehicles road bound. Staying on main roads and paths, however, made the tanks easy targets for the Germans' preplanned antitank defense. Panzers and 88-mm antitank guns were sited to take advantage of long fields of fire and covered highways, bridges, and road junctions. Indirect fires were preplanned to strike American armor moving along highways. Early in the campaign, tankers attempted to execute massed attacks in columns down the Normandy highways—blitz actions that were ineffective and costly. The Germans stopped a typical American tank attack on 15 June, as an armored unit supported the U.S. 120th Infantry of the 30th Infantry Division during an attack southward from Omaha Beach. The American tanks never left the road, while the accompanying infantry operated on the flanks. Within moments, the Germans destroyed the three lead tanks, one immobilized by a mine and two others hit by an 88-mm antitank gun, and the attack ground to a confused halt. Armor leaders soon realized that tanks had to stay off highways to survive. Their only alternative was to operate within the cover and concealment of the hedgerows.[15]

Army doctrine for the coordinated use of tanks and infantry was ineffective in the Bocage. The hedgerows' earthen embankments and heavy vegetation were almost impassable obstacles for the M-4 Shermans. Tanks could not lead the attack through the hedgerows nor support leading infantry attacks with main-gun and machine-gun fire. Unable to operate through the hedgerows with attacking infantrymen, tanks had to take a passive role and merely followed the main infantry attack, while awaiting suitable opportunities for employment.

Another serious problem that became evident during the early Normandy battles was that tank-infantry coordination was poor. Insufficient combined arms training had been conducted before D-Day. Primarily concerned with the problems of amphibious warfare, infantry divisions failed to train adequately with their assigned tank units. Another difficulty was that supporting GHQ tank battalions were not assigned to their respective infantry divisions until a few weeks prior to D-Day. For example, the 745th Tank Battalion was not assigned to the 1st Infantry Division until 21 April, and tank companies were not attached to individual infantry regiments until they were already in combat after D-Day.[16]

Another cause for poor tank-infantry coordination was that many infantry commanders had not worked with tanks before and lacked sufficient experience concerning how tanks should be used in conjunction with infantry. The exact details of how tanks and infantry should work together were largely neglected until infantrymen and tankers found themselves thrown together among the hedgerows. Many commanders at the battalion level and above were inexperienced in integrating the components of the combined arms team. The operations officer of Collins' VII Corps elaborated on this problem: "More combined training for infantry battalion commanders is needed. They should know how to use all of their tools. . . . We have had to teach this in battle the hard way. The same also applies to regimental commanders."[17]

A bright spot in the American combined arms teams was the field artillery. Infantry commanders understood artillery doctrine and knew how to best employ their supporting fires. Infantry-artillery coordination was consistently good throughout First Army. When conditions permitted, artillery wreaked havoc on the enemy. German prisoners consistently stated that U.S. artillery fire was extremely effective. Captured officers with experience in Russia believed that American artillery was more powerful and devastating than Soviet artillery.[18]

Despite the outstanding performance of the infantry-artillery team, several conditions inhibited artillery operations. Ammunition shortages, for one, plagued First Army artillery units throughout the Normandy campaign. Lack of positions from which to observe targets also compelled artillery batteries to fire on unobserved targets and unconfirmed locations of German units. Inadequate observation also restricted counterbattery fires against German artillery and harassing and interdiction fires against targets in the German rear.[19]

The central challenge facing U.S. commanders in Normandy, however, was how to rupture the hedgerow defenses and get their own units moving quickly forward instead of systematically grinding their way through the Germans' prepared positions. Since the hedgerows and the confined spaces within the beachhead precluded outflanking maneuvers, the only available alternative was the least desirable one: frontal assaults straight into the enemy's kill zones. American commanders at all levels understood that answers to tactical problems had to be found before a stalemate ensued. Methods and techniques had to be devised that would overcome the hedgerow barriers, degrade the German defense, and restore the initiative to the attacker. First Army realized it could not afford the luxury of suspending operations to repair deficiencies in the combined arms team or to determine the very best way of busting the German defenses. Solutions to these problems would have to be found and implemented in the midst of battle.

The Solution

By late June, most commanders throughout First Army realized the peculiar nature of the fighting taking place in the hedgerows. From a tactical standpoint, hedgerow combat was unlike anything the Americans had ever before encountered. Combat consisted of small-unit actions aimed at reducing the German positions in each field rather than sweeping maneuvers to seize major objectives. Veterans with experience in North Africa and Sicily had not encountered anything comparable to the Normandy hedgerows. Similarly, combat training did not prepare unblooded soldiers for the tactical problems unique to hedgerow fighting. Battle in Normandy put a higher premium on leadership and initiative at the small-unit level rather than on generalship. Some commanders compared the hedgerow fighting to combat in jungles or forests. Others said it was more akin to Indian fighting.[20]

The leaders within First Army realized they had to find ways to smash through the German defenses. Unable to outflank enemy positions, American soldiers had to find ways to restore tactical mobility and to bring more heavy-caliber weapons to bear against the Germans. As they tried to develop techniques that would succeed within the confined spaces of the Bocage, commanders gleaned little help from Army doctrine or standard tactical procedures. Nonetheless, as early as 9 June, First Army headquarters began to grapple with the problem of how to get through the hedgerows. In a conversation with an armor officer on First Army's staff, General Bradley wondered whether tanks could blow their way through the hedgerows with main-gun and machine-gun fires. Throughout First Army during June and July, officers, noncommissioned officers, and enlisted men contemplated methods to overcome the German defense.[21]

The most obvious solution to the problems of hedgerow combat was for American commanders to find ways to maximize the advantages of the tools most readily available to them: the mobility and firepower of the combined arms team. The key challenge to the U.S. Army was to finds ways to bring the separate components of the combined arms teams together in a concerted attack against the German hedgerow defenses. Infantry, armor, and artillery had to be knitted together into an effective fighting team.

Early in the campaign, infantry commanders realized that before their units could maneuver to close with the enemy, they had to find a way to deliver heavy suppressive fires against the Germans. The most obvious solution at hand was to better integrate armor into the attack so as to capitalize on their tanks' armored protection and firepower. Instead of attacking in separate echelons as prescribed in doctrinal manuals, infantry and armor had to be able to advance simultaneously in the face of German defenses, while mutually supporting one another. If tanks and infantry worked closely together, infantrymen might be able to assault the Germans while Shermans delivered heavy suppressive fire with their machine guns and cannon.[22]

However, before infantrymen and tankers could operate together in the hedgerows, several technical problems had to be solved. The most pressing and difficult problem was to find ways for the First Army's M-4 Shermans to overcome the physical barrier presented by the hedgerows. Another obstacle to tank-infantry coordination was inadequate communications. If ways could be found for the Shermans to bash through the hedgerows and communicate with their accompanying infantry, tanks would be able to deliver suppressive firepower and help the infantry move forward.

The search for a solution to the armored mobility problem typifies the problem-solving processes that took place throughout First Army. Tank units discovered that Shermans could drive over the top of smaller hedgerows. Negotiating larger hedgerows was a hazardous, if not impossible, task and exposed the tanks' thin underbellies to antitank fire. The first attempts at penetrating the hedgerows involved the use of specially equipped "dozer" tanks. These tanks were a relatively new invention in 1944 and consisted of M-4 Shermans equipped with a blade similar to those on commercial bulldozers. Dozer tanks normally removed obstacles or improved defensive positions. Early experience in Normandy showed that a dozer tank could push its way through the most formidable hedgerow. Dozer tanks could also widen natural gaps in hedgerows that were too narrow for Shermans to drive through.[23]

However, there were too few dozer tanks in First Army to support large-scale operations on wide frontages. A tank battalion was usually equipped with only four dozer tanks. These tanks were too few in number to support divisional attacks effectively where each infantry regiment might encounter dozens of hedgerows. To alleviate the situation, armor leaders recommended that one tank in each armor platoon be equipped with a blade device. First Army made frantic efforts to increase the number of its dozer tanks. In July 1944, First Army requisitioned

278 dozer blades. However, units could not sit idly by while waiting for supply channels to produce the badly needed dozer blades. Weeks might pass before enough dozer tanks became available to allow widespread armor operations through the hedgerows.[24]

The urgency of the situation resulted in the development of improvised methods that allowed tanks to maneuver in the Bocage. The first field-expedient solution to the mobility problem came from the 747th Tank Battalion assigned to Major General Charles H. Gerhardt's 29th Infantry Division. The 747th was not equipped with dozer tanks, so instead of trying to drive directly over the hedgerows, someone suggested that demolitions be used to blow gaps in the hedgerows. After experimentation, the tankers discovered that demolitions could indeed breach the hedgerows. Two 24-pound explosive charges placed eight feet apart and eighteen inches above ground level blew a sizable hole in a hedgerow. On 24 June, engineer squads from the 29th Division's 121st Engineer Combat Battalion emplaced demolition charges on hedgerows during a limited attack by elements of the 747th Tank Battalion and the 115th Infantry. The attackers discovered that the 24-pound charges did not always create a hole large enough for the Shermans. After the attack, the engineers decided to increase the size of the explosive charges from twenty-four to fifty pounds. They hoped the increased charges would consistently blow breaches large enough to accommodate the attacking tanks.[25]

However, several problems resulted from increasing the size and weight of the explosive charges. The commander of the 121st Engineer Combat Battalion, Lieutenant Colonel Robert R. Ploger, conducted an informal study of the logistics involved in supporting a tank attack with fifty-pound explosive charges. Ploger assumed that in a typical attack, a tank company moving a distance of one and one-half miles through the Bocage would encounter thirty-four separate hedgerows. As a result, each tank company needed seventeen tons of explosives. Demolitions were not readily available in such quantities, and the problems involved in the transport and emplacement of enough explosives seemed insurmountable. Apparently, other techniques were needed to breach the hedgerows.[26]

The engineers then suggested that the explosives be buried within the hedgerow embankments. Burying the charges would greatly increase the efficiency of the demolitions, allow the use of smaller charges, and alleviate problems associated with availability, transport, and emplacement. Unfortunately, other conditions prevented the burying of explosive charges. Digging holes large and deep enough for the explosives in earthen embankments covered with vines and filled with roots proved too laborious. During an attack, digging holes and emplacing charges would simply take too long. Since an attack could proceed only as fast as charges were emplaced and detonated, slow-moving American attacks would allow the Germans to coordinate their hedgerow defense better. Engineers and infantrymen would also be dangerously exposed to German mortar fire while planting demolitions. Though technically feasible, burying explosives by hand was a procedure both too difficult and tactically unwise.[27]

Determined to find a way to get through the hedgerows, the tankers and engineers finally developed an effective technique for using explosives. In a conference between officers of the 747th Tank Battalion and Lieutenant Colonel Ploger, someone suggested that the tanks be equipped with a mechanical device to gouge holes in the hedgerows for the explosives. After some experimentation, the tankers finally equipped an M-4 Sherman with two pieces of commercial pipe, each four feet long and six and one-half inches in diameter. The tankers welded the pipes onto the front side of the Sherman's final drive assemblies and reinforced the weld with angle irons. Shermans so equipped simply rammed into a hedgerow embankment and then backed away leaving two sizable holes for the explosives. Ploger's engineers also learned to pack the demolitions into expended 105-mm artillery shell casings, thereby greatly increasing the efficiency of the charges. The engineers found that two charges of only fifteen pounds each could blow a gap large enough for a Sherman tank. Placing explosives in shell casings also made the transport and handling of charges much easier. The method proved so successful that the 747th outfitted numerous tanks with the pipe devices.[28]

Several factors soon led to an even better method of breaching the hedgerows. The tankers discovered that demolitions took away the element of surprise during attacks. An explosion alerted the Germans that a tank would soon appear through the hedgerows. The detonation clearly marked where the tank would appear, thus forming an aiming point for German machine-gun and antitank fires. A method that did not use explosives would increase the effectiveness of American attacks by restoring the element of surprise.[29]

During experiments to test the feasibility of the pipe devices, the tankers of the 747th discovered that a Sherman equipped with pipes could sometimes plough its own way through smaller hedgerows. Unfortunately, the maneuver frequently bent the pipes or tore them loose from the tank. After observing that tanks with pipes could penetrate some hedgerows on their own, First Lieutenant Charles B. Green of the 747th designed a strong bumper device for use in plowing through the hedgerows. Made from salvaged railroad tracks, the new tank bumper proved strong enough to tear through almost any hedgerow. After proving successful in combat, maintenance teams welded the bumper onto many of the 747th's Shermans.[30]

By late June, many units throughout First Army had developed a variety of means to breach the hedgerows. The 83d Infantry Division in VII Corps used two 25-pound explosive charges. Engineers packed the explosives in a sandbag, buried them by hand two feet into the hedgerow embankment, and then tamped the hole full of dirt to increase the effectiveness of the charge. Other units copied the techniques developed in the 29th Division. The 703d Tank Battalion, attached to the 4th Infantry Division in VII Corps, adopted the 747th's hedgerow-busting techniques and found them "highly successful." In VIII Corps, the 79th Infantry Division also developed another type of hedgerow cutter for use on its Sherman tanks.[31]

Soldiers of the 2d Armored Division's 102d Cavalry Reconnaissance Squadron invented the hedgerow device that gained the widest publicity. During a discussion between some of the 102d's officers and enlisted men, someone suggested that they get "saw teeth," put them on their tanks, and cut through the hedgerows. Many of the troops laughed at the suggestion, but Sergeant Curtis G. Culin took the idea to heart. Culin designed and supervised the construction of a hedgerow cutting device made from scrap iron pulled from a German roadblock. Testing showed that the device allowed a Sherman to cut easily through the hedgerows. Because the hedgerow cutter's blades made a tank resemble a large pachyderm with tusks, troops called the device a "rhinoceros," and Shermans equipped with Culin's invention became known as "rhino" tanks. Though the most famous of the hedgerow-reducing devices, Culin's "rhinoceros" was only one of many such contrivances invented and employed throughout First Army.[32]

Culin's device soon got the attention of the chain of command within 2d Armored Division and V Corps. On 14 July, General Bradley attended a demonstration of Culin's hedgerow cutter. Bradley watched as Shermans mounting the hedgerow device plowed through the hedgerows "as though they were

A close-up view of a typical hedgerow-cutter device

pasteboard, throwing the bushes and brush into the air." Very impressed by the demonstration, Bradley ordered the chief of First Army's Ordnance Section to supervise the construction and installation of as many of the hedgerow cutters as possible.[33]

First Army Ordnance assembled welders and welding equipment within the beachhead and from the rear areas in England to assist with the project. Welding teams used scrap metal from German beach obstacles to construct most of the hedgerow cutters. In a prodigious effort between 14—25 July, the First Army Ordnance Section produced over 500 hedgerow cutters and distributed them to subordinate commands for installation. By late July, 60 percent of First Army's Shermans mounted the hedgerow-cutting devices.[34]

Another problem besetting the U.S. Army in the early stages of the campaign was inadequate communications, which prevented close coordination between tankers and infantrymen. The din of battle and roar of tank engines drowned out voice communications between tank commanders and troops on the ground. Infantrymen could not get the attention of tankers who were busy inside their vehicles. The most significant problem was that the majority of tank and infantry radios operated on different wavelengths. Such incompatible equipment made direct radio communications between tanks and infantry platoons impossible. Out of the seven radios authorized in an infantry company, only the company commander's radio transmitted and received with tank radios. Conversely, in a tank platoon only the platoon leader and the platoon sergeant had radios capable of communicating with an infantry company commander's radio. Unable to communicate during combat, infantry squads and tankers failed to coordinate their fires against the Germans.[35]

Eventually, soldiers devised several field-expedient solutions to communications problems. One technique involved the attachment of two infantry field telephones to each tank. Infantrymen strapped one phone onto the rear of a Sherman's back deck and then connected it by wire to a second phone located inside the tank's turret. By using such back-deck telephones, soldiers could direct tankers against concealed German positions. However, infantrymen were forced to expose themselves to enemy fire while talking on the back-deck telephones. Some units tried to solve the problem by letting a long strand of communications wire trail behind the tanks. Infantrymen then connected a field telephone to the end of the trailing wires and talked with the tank's crews from a safer position. However, dangling wires often accidentally broke, pulled loose from the tanks, or got entangled in the tanks' treads. Infantrymen and tank crews discovered the best way to communicate was through the tanks' interphone boxes, which were connected directly into the tanks' intercom systems, and were then mounted on each Sherman's back deck in empty ammunition containers. To talk with the tankers, infantrymen simply plugged a radio handset into the interphone boxes. The handsets' long cords permitted soldiers to lie down behind or underneath the tanks to protect themselves while talking to the tank crews. By mid-July, many divisions in First Army used field-expedient methods for communications between tanks and supporting infantrymen.[36]

Units also found ways to facilitate better radio communications. Both tank and infantry units tried to increase the span of control by procuring additional radios. Tank platoon leaders in some units acquired extra, manpack armor radios for use by the infantry. Other tank units tried to install infantry radios in their vehicles but with poor results. A popular method of increasing command and control by radio was for infantry commanders to ride in the command vehicle of the attached armor unit. By riding in a command tank and using a manpack infantry radio, a rifle company commander could simultaneously control the movement of his platoons and attached tanks.[37]

Troops developed a wide variety of visual signals and standing operating procedures to coordinate actions during battle. Because tankers and infantrymen used different standard hand and arm signals, soldiers had to develop new signals for various functions. Tank-infantry teams invented signals for "commence fire," "cease fire," and to indicate the location of enemy positions. Leaders also used smoke grenades and flares to control their subordinates. Many infantry squad and platoon leaders carried rifles that fired tracer bullets used to mark targets. Infantry commanders learned to assign the same squads to work with supporting tanks and found that familiarity between tank crews and infantry squads greatly increased the soldiers' confidence and proficiency.[38]

Inadequate observation of artillery targets was also a problem that hampered combined arms operations. Operating in the flat hedgerow thickets, forward observers lacked adequate fields of observation to adjust fire onto German forward positions or targets in the enemy's rear. A shortage of forward observers also hampered operations. Artillery battalions normally assigned one forward observer to each rifle platoon in an infantry company, while tank companies received only one forward observer for use by the company commander. Because tank companies rarely operated as a single unit, tank platoons did not have their own means of calling for fire. Normally tankers sent their requests for fire to the forward observer of their accompanying infantry unit—usually without results. Tank platoon leaders sometimes called for fire by communicating directly with the fire-direction center of their supporting artillery. Unfortunately, armor officers were often incapable of sending correct calls for fire or could not adjust rounds onto targets.[39]

Aerial forward observers were the best solution to the problems of observing enemy targets. In First Army, each division had ten light aircraft assigned for liaison missions, and each corps headquarters had from fifty to seventy aircraft. The airplanes were either L-4 Piper Cubs or the larger L-5 Stinson Sentinels. Besides the pilot, the aircraft carried a skilled forward observer equipped with radios linked to the fire-direction centers of supporting artillery units. Loitering over a designated sector, aerial forward observers called fire on forward enemy positions and valuable targets in the German rear area and adjusted barrages in support of American ground attacks. During the Normandy battles, aerial forward observers conducted the majority of target-fire missions with "universally excellent" results.[40]

Aerial observers also performed numerous other functions. On several occasions, observers adjusted artillery fire to neutralize German gun positions firing on American fighter-bombers engaged in close air support missions. During VII Corps' attack on Cherbourg, air observers adjusted naval gunfire for ground units. Whenever observer aircraft were in the area, German artillery batteries were reluctant to fire for fear of revealing their location and exposing themselves to American counter-battery fire. Air observers also collected tactical intelligence by taking photographs that ground units used in preparing for attacks. The small aircraft were reliable, highly maneuverable, and surprisingly survivable; only nine Piper Cubs were lost during operations in Normandy.[41]

Technical innovations in mobility, communications, and artillery observation were not enough to ensure a coordinated combined arms effort. Small-unit tactics also had to be developed so that indirect fire pounded the enemy while closely coordinated teams of tanks and infantry assaulted German defensive positions. With the problems of armored mobility and tactical communications largely solved, infantry commanders finally realized that firepower from their supporting M-4 Shermans could place heavy suppressive fires on the Germans, thus allowing their units a chance to maneuver. Properly employed, the machine guns of an M-4 Sherman delivered the direct fire needed to suppress German machine guns, while a Sherman's main gun, used at point-blank range, substituted for indirect artillery fire. As tanks suppressed the German defenders, infantry units could clear out the hedgerows and maneuver to assault the main German defensive positions. Infantry could also provide tanks with protection against German close assaults. Throughout First Army, units worked to develop new combined arms tactics. Commanders at all levels began to experiment with methods that permitted infantry and tanks to work closely together. Units trained and conducted rehearsals in rear areas before trying new tactics in combat. The result was the implementation by First Army units of several methods that allowed the combined arms team to overcome the enemy.

Events within the 29th Infantry Division best illustrate how the U.S. Army developed and executed new tactical methods. In an attempt to expand the Normandy beachhead, First Army ordered Corlett's XIX Corps to attack the Germans on 16 June and seize prominent terrain north and east of Saint-Lô. The XIX Corps ordered Gerhardt's 29th Division to conduct the main attack and to take key terrain near the villages of Saint-André-de-l'Epine and Villiers-Fossard (see map 2). The attack jumped off early on the morning of 16 June and failed to make any substantial progress against the Germans. By late afternoon, it was obvious that the 29th Division's regiments would not reach their initial objectives before nightfall. Major General Corlett issued orders for the forward troops to dig in for the night and to prepare to resume the attack the next day. The 29th Division continued to attack for two more days but with few beneficial results. By nightfall on 18 June, the division was exhausted, bloodied, and unable to continue the attack. In this instance, the German hedgerow defense had successfully stopped the best American efforts to smash through the Bocage.[42]

Other operations in the 29th Division's sector also exhibited deficiencies in tank-infantry coordination. An attack on 20 June by the 175th Infantry and Company B, 747th Tank Battalion, against German positions near Villiers-Fossard demonstrated the problems of operating among the hedgerows. Using standard tank-infantry tactics, the tankers led the attack, and the infantry followed. Tankers and infantrymen, however, failed to support one another during the attack and soon became separated, as the tankers blew the hedgerows with explosives and plunged forward alone. German machine guns pinned down the infantry, while the unescorted American tanks soon fell prey to German antitank fires. Company B lost four tanks in the attack, and finally both tankers and infantrymen had to withdraw to their initial positions.[43]

Frustrated by their failures in the hedgerows, leaders within the 29th Division realized they had to find ways to defeat the Germans. General Gerhardt directed the assistant division commander, Brigadier General Norman D. Cota, to supervise the development and implementation of tactics to overcome the German method of hedgerow defense. The tactics developed by the 29th Division were a departure from normal Army doctrine in that neither the tanks nor the infantry led the attack but fought closely together and protected one another while closing with the enemy.[44]

The 29th Division's solution relied on the firepower and maneuver of small, closely coordinated combat teams. Each team consisted of a single tank, an engineer team, and a squad of infantry reinforced by a light machine gun and a 60-mm mortar from an infantry company's weapons platoon. Before the attack, the infantry and engineers occupied the hedgerow that served as the jump-off position for the assault (see figure 3). The attack began when a Sherman equipped with pipe devices nosed into the hedgerow and opened fire on the Germans with main gun and machine guns. The Sherman first fired a white phosphorous round into the corners of the opposite hedgerow to eliminate German heavy machine-gun positions. The tankers then systematically sprayed machine-gun fire along the entire base of the enemy hedgerow. The 60-mm mortar supported the attack by lobbing shells into the fields directly behind the German positions. The infantry attacked when the Sherman opened fire with its machine guns. The squad moved through the hedgerow deployed on line and advanced across the open field using standard methods of fire and movement. The infantry stayed away from the hedgerows on their flanks to avoid enemy grazing fire. The Sherman continued to support the attack until the infantry's advance masked the tank's machine-gun fire. As they closed on the German positions, American infantrymen threw hand grenades over the hedgerow to kill or confuse German defenders on the opposite side. Simultaneously, the Sherman backed away from its firing position, and the engineers emplaced demolitions in the holes left by the Sherman's pipe devices. After the explosives blew a hole in the hedgerow, the Sherman moved forward to provide close support to the infantry squad. The tankers and infantrymen then flushed the hedgerow of any remaining defenders and prepared to continue the attack. The engineer team and machine-gun and mortar crews then displaced forward to support the next assault.[45]

On 24 June, elements of the 29th Division conducted a full rehearsal in the division rear area to test the validity of the new close-assault tactics. An infantry platoon, a tank platoon, and three engineer teams rehearsed the new tactics during several simulated attacks. Lessons learned during the exercise helped improve the effectiveness of the hedgerow tactics. The infantry discovered a light machine gun could not be moved quickly enough to keep up with their advance. Instead, the infantry preferred to use Browning automatic rifles to provide suppressive fire. Infantrymen also learned to coordinate their attack with tankers by using rear-deck telephones mounted on the backs of the Shermans. Mortar observers discovered that by standing on the Sherman's rear deck, they could see the next hedgerow and adjust rounds onto the German positions. Mortar crews also learned they could help protect the assaulting

Phase I

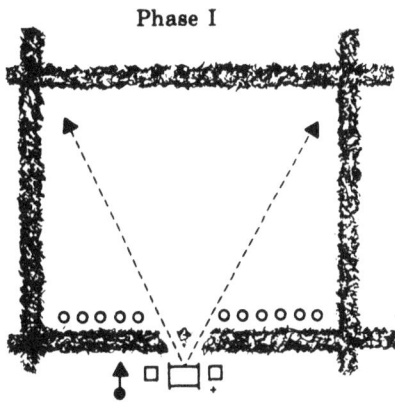

Tank lays down suppressive fire as infantry moves through hedgerow.

Phase II

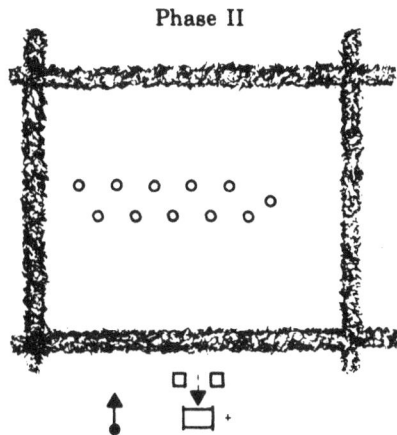

As infantry close on enemy and mask tank's fire, tank backs away and engineers emplace charges.

Phase III

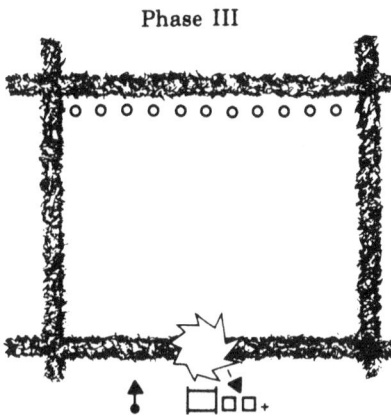

Demolitions gap hedgerow as infantry assaults the objective.

Phase IV

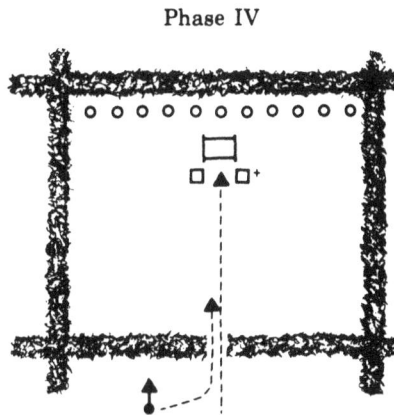

Tank advances to help infantry clear objectives. Other elements displace forward and prepare to continue the attack.

LEGEND

☐	Sherman tank	☐	Engineer team
●	60-mm mortar	o o	Infantrymen
		+	Mortar observer

Figure 3. The 29th Infantry Division's hedgerow tactics

Courtesy Dwight D. Eisenhower Library

A Sherman tank crew practices using a hedgerow-cutter device prior to a battle

infantry squad by obscuring German observation with smoke shells. The tankers found out that crew members had to dismount and cut away vegetation to clear adequate fields of fire and observation. The rehearsals made tank commanders realize they had to control their machine-gun fire closely to avoid hitting friendly infantrymen.[46]

After the rehearsal on 24 June, the 29th Division's operations staff prepared diagrams and explanatory notes outlining the new hedgerow tactics in detail. The operations section then distributed the information as a training memorandum to all regiments within the division. Units in the 29th Division practiced and rehearsed the new tactics in preparation for their next bout with the Germans.[47] On 1 July, General Cota summed up the 29th Division's tactical experience in France:

> What held us up at first was that we originally were organized to assault the beach, suffered a lot of casualties among key men, then hit another kind of warfare for which we were not organized. We had to assemble replacements and reorganize. Now we have had time to reorganize and give this warfare some thought. I think we will go next time.[48]

The 29th Division did not have to wait long for an opportunity to use its new combined arms tactics.

On 11 July, XIX Corps attacked southward toward Saint-Lô as part of a First Army offensive to push the German Seventh Army out of Normandy. The XIX Corps ordered the 29th Division to attack and seize key terrain east of Saint-Lô. As part of the division's attack plan, General Gerhardt ordered the 116th Infantry to conduct the main attack and capture Saint-André-de-l'Epine, then swing westward and attack along a major ridge-line to take the village of Martinville (see map 2). The regimental commander then ordered the 2d Battalion, 116th Infantry, to lead the attack with the other battalions following in column. Company B of the 121st Engineer Combat Battalion and Company A of the 747th Tank Battalion supported the 2d Battalion. The lead battalion planned to execute the attack with two rifle companies that had been trained and organized to execute the 29th Division's new hedgerow tactics.[49]

The attack started at 0600 on 11 July after a furious twenty-minute preparatory bombardment by five battalions of artillery. Initial progress was slow and discouraging. The 2d Battalion advanced with two companies abreast and encountered determined resistance from enemy positions in the first hedgerows. The tank-infantry-engineer teams, however, continued to push forward, and by 1100 they finally broke through the organized German defense, which eased and then collapsed. The 2d Battalion then made rapid progress, seized the ridgeline to its front, wheeled to the right, and continued to move. Before nightfall, the 2d Battalion advanced another mile toward Martinville and was in an excellent position to continue the attack toward Saint-Lô.[50]

The 116th Infantry's attack demonstrated the effectiveness of the 29th Division's hedgerow tactics. Compared to other operations in the Bocage, the 2d Battalion's advance made spectacular progress. The battalion achieved a major penetration of the enemy line and completely ruptured the main line of German resistance. General Gerhardt attributed the success to tank-infantry-engineer teamwork. Mortars delivered fire on the German positions, tanks provided suppressive fire, engineers breached the hedgerows, and infantry assaulted the Germans while protecting the Shermans against antitank fires. Infantry casualties were relatively light during the attack, and not one Sherman was lost.[51]

Major General Walter M. Robertson's 2d Infantry Division in V Corps had a similar experience with hedgerow combat.

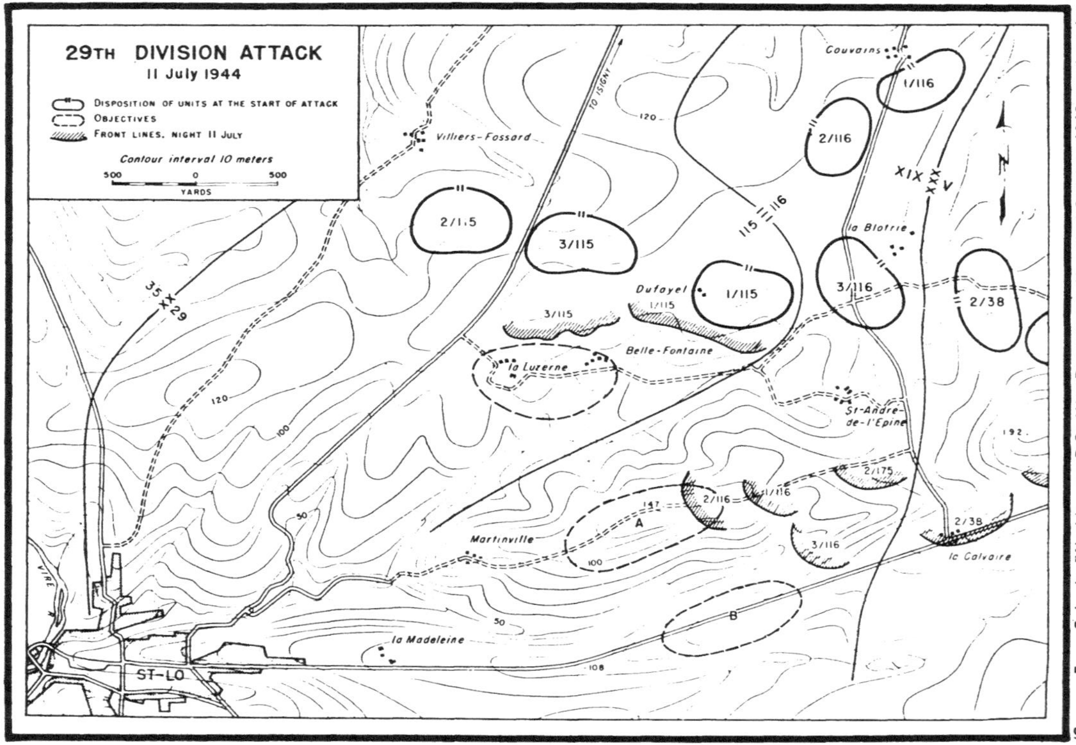

44

29TH DIVISION ATTACK
11 July 1944

Disposition of units at the start of attack
Objectives
Front lines, night 11 July

Contour interval 10 meters

500   0   500
YARDS

Map 2. The 29th Division's attack, 11 July 1944

During 12—16 June, the 2d Division battered itself against Hill 192, the highest terrain feature in the Saint-Lô area, which allowed the Germans to observe all major activities within the entire V and XIX Corps sectors. Hill 192 was also one of the most heavily defended German strongpoints in the entire First Army sector. After repeated assaults over a four-day period, the division failed to take Hill 192 and suffered 1,253 casualties.[52]

In the aftermath of the June attacks, the 2d Division began to look for successful ways to attack through the hedgerows. The tactics they developed and employed varied slightly from the procedures used in the 29th Division. In small-unit actions, engineer teams accompanied each Sherman tank as well as each infantry squad. Once the infantry squad attacked and secured an enemy hedgerow, the accompanying engineers immediately began to prepare the hedgerow for demolition. Engineers with the Sherman gapped the hedgerow holding up the tank and then swept a path for the tank through the open field with mine detectors. Two infantrymen provided constant local security for the Sherman. Follow-on infantry platoons actively probed the hedgerows to look for concealed Germans and to eliminate snipers.[53]

As part of the major offensive of 11 July, First Army ordered V Corps to attack and seize the dominating terrain east of Saint-Lô. General Gerow ordered the 2d Division to once again attack and seize Hill 192. General Robertson ordered the 38th Infantry to conduct the main attack. This time, the regimental commander decided to conduct a powerful frontal assault with two battalions abreast.[54]

The attack started at 0630 on 11 July after a devastating twenty-minute artillery bombardment (see map 3). The 1st and 2d Battalions led the attack, supported by two tank companies from the 741st Tank Battalion and an engineer company from the 2d Engineer Combat Battalion. The Germans put up stiff resistance from the beginning. One tank company lost six Shermans to German *panzerfausts*. Fanatical Germans defending a position near "Kraut Corner" refused to surrender and were run over and buried alive by one of the 741st's dozer tanks. However, the 38th Infantry began to make good progress by using its new hedgerow tactics. Devastating artillery fire closely supported the infantry advance by maintaining heavy barrages in front of the attacking units. Around noon, the 38th Infantry finally reached the top of Hill 192 as the Germans disengaged and withdrew to the south. By nightfall, the 38th Infantry had

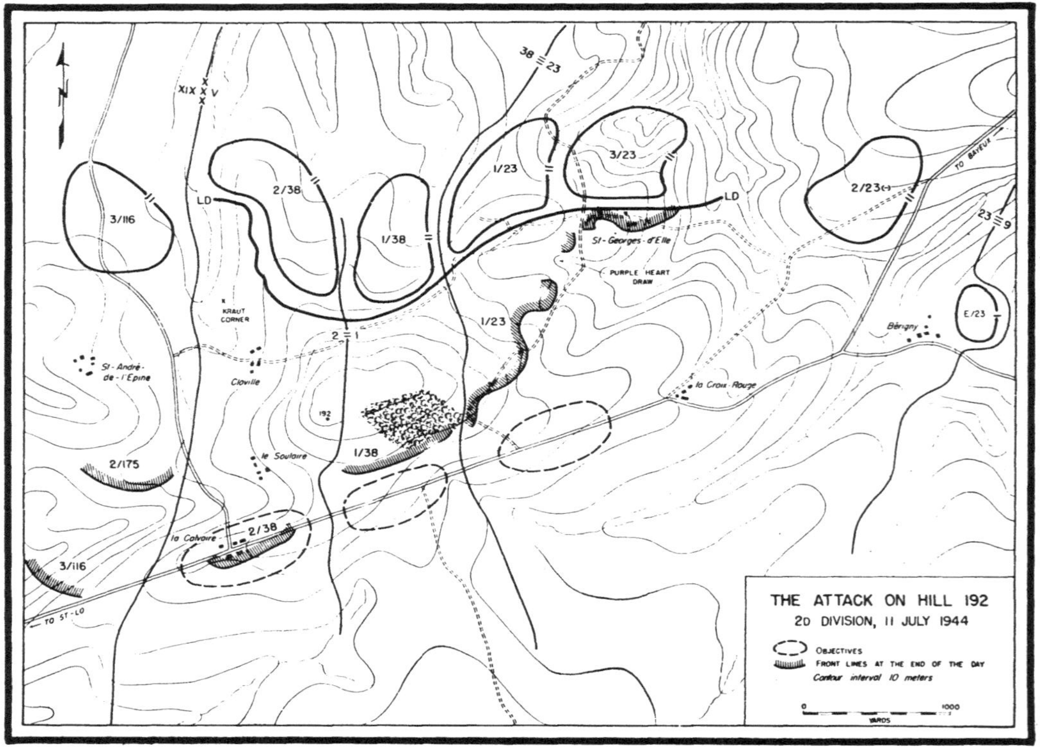

Map 3. The attack on Hill 192, 11 July 1944

(Source: From *Saint-Lo* [Washington, D.C.: War Department, Historical Division, 1946; reprint ed., Washington, D.C.: U.S. Army, Center of Military History, 1984], p. 59.)

cleared Hill 192 of all German defenders and was well entrenched in positions on the hill's southern slopes.[55]

Like the 29th Division's attack against the Martinville ridge,
the 2d Division's attack was an outstanding success. The
principal reason was the proper use of tank-infantry-engineer
teams. The infantry found that the tank's rear-deck telephones
helped greatly in coordinating the attack. One battalion commander reported that because of the new hedgerow tactics, his
battalion lost no troops to sniper fire, while in previous operations snipers had caused over 50 percent of all casualties. A
second reason for the success on 11 July was the awesome firepower of American artillery. The 2d Division's own artillery
units fired 20,000 rounds in support of the attack. All together,
American artillery battalions dumped forty-five tons of high
explosives on the Germans defending Hill 192.[56]

The 83d Infantry Division in Collins' VII Corps also devised
other techniques for attacking through the hedgerows. Arriving
in Normandy in late June, the 83d Division, commanded by
Major General Robert C. Macon, relieved the battle-weary 101st
Airborne Division and then occupied static defensive positions
near Carentan. While awaiting commitment to offensive operations, the 83d Division drew from the 101st Airborne's battle
experiences to develop small-unit tactics for use in the hedgerows.[57]

As in other divisions, the 83d Division's combined arms
tactics capitalized on the complementary fire and maneuver of
tank-infantry-engineer teams supported by mortars and artillery.
The attacking elements consisted of an infantry squad, an
engineer team, and a tank section (see figure 4). The attack
opened when the lead Sherman, positioned along a hedgerow
with the infantry and the engineers, opened fire with its main
gun against the German heavy machine-gun positions in the
corners of the opposite hedgerow. Simultaneously, the infantry
fired from their positions with their own small arms. In addition,
supporting mortars lobbed rounds on the first defensive position,
while artillery shelled German defensive positions in depth. After
the lead Sherman thoroughly covered the opposite hedgerow
with main-gun and machine-gun fire, the assault began. The
engineers gapped the hedgerow with buried explosive charges,
as the infantry squad pushed forward through the hedgerow.
As soon as the hedgerow was breached, the second Sherman
moved forward through the gap and attacked across the open
field with the infantry, while the support tank continued to fire

48

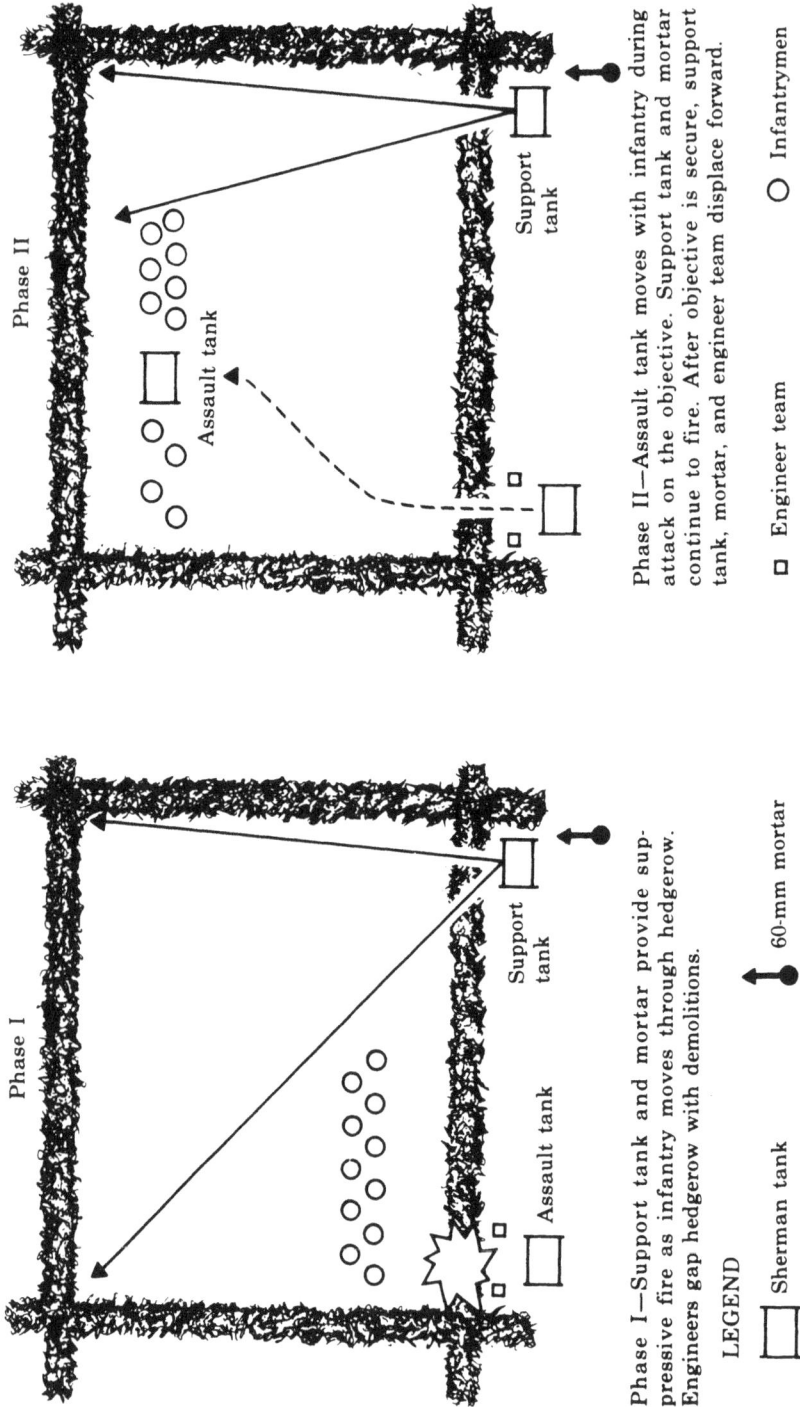

Phase II—Assault tank moves with infantry during attack on the objective. Support tank and mortar continue to fire. After objective is secure, support tank, mortar, and engineer team displace forward.

Phase I—Support tank and mortar provide suppressive fire as infantry moves through hedgerow. Engineers gap hedgerow with demolitions.

LEGEND

☐ Sherman tank

◖ 60-mm mortar

☐ Engineer team

○ Infantrymen

Figure 4. The 83d Infantry Division's hedgerow tactics

The combined arms team in action. By the end of the Normandy campaign, close-knit teams of tanks and infantry were common throughout First Army

from its initial position. At the height of the attack, maximum firepower from mortars, a rifle squad, and two Sherman tanks simultaneously assailed the Germans. After the assaulting tank and infantry squad secured the enemy hedgerow, the supporting Sherman, the engineer team, and the mortar crews displaced forward to prepare for the next operation. The assault tank then became the support tank for the next attack.[58]

During the last days of June, units in the 83d Division underwent rigorous training to prepare for combat in the hedgerows. The division was untested in battle and had almost no experience in working with tanks. Each unit received training in hedgerow tactics from small, combined arms instruction teams formed at division level. Troops from the 101st Airborne and 2d Armored Divisions with experience in hedgerow warfare helped train the 83d Division's tank-infantry-engineer teams.[59]

Despite rigorous training and preparation, the 83d Division's introduction into combat was a bloody failure and illustrates what occurred when American units failed to coordinate their efforts. On 4 July, the 83d Division, supported by the 746th

Tank Battalion, attacked southward from Carentan, with the mission of seizing a vital road junction at the village of Périers (see map 3). Due to low, wet ground in the sector, the 83d Division had to attack with two regiments abreast along a narrow strip of high ground on both sides of the main Carentan-Périers highway. The restricted avenue of advance greatly assisted German units in defending the sector. From the beginning, bad luck and weather plagued the attack. Despite their intensive prebattle training, inexperienced units disintegrated as they tried to execute their hedgerow assault tactics. Tank-infantry coordination was particularly poor and resulted in violent outbursts between tankers and infantrymen. At least one infantry commander threatened to shoot an armor officer for failing to support an attack, and one tank commander threatened to gun down infantrymen who provided inadequate local security for his vehicle. Unable to root out the Germans with uncoordinated attacks, the division's offensive came to a complete, bloody halt. The 83d Division paid a heavy price for its clumsy and confused attack. By nightfall on 5 July, the division had advanced only 1,600 yards while suffering 2,100 casualties.[60]

Armored divisions also studied how best to attack through the Bocage. The lead elements of 3d Armored Division arrived in Normandy in late June and were assigned to XIX Corps. By 29 June, 3d Armored Division's Combat Command A (CCA), commanded by Brigadier General Doyle O. Hickey and consisting of the 32d Armored Regiment and the 36th Armored Infantry Regiment, was ready for combat. As troops arrived in France, Hickey's staff and some of his unit commanders talked to Corlett's XIX Corps staff about operations in the Bocage. Based on the previous combat experiences of XIX Corps' units, the tankers decided to develop their own special tactics for combat in the hedgerows.[61]

In late June, 3d Armored Division devised hedgerow tactics that emphasized coordinated, combined efforts by tanks and infantry. Again, mobility and firepower were the key elements in the tactical formula. Like other units in First Army, 3d Armored Division discovered that dozer tanks and engineer teams with demolitions could breach the most formidable hedgerows. Tank platoons operating with infantry squads and supported by artillery and mortar fire were expected to deliver enough direct firepower to root out the most determined defenders.[62]

Unlike infantry divisions that developed hedgerow tactics for single tanks and infantry squads, 3d Armored Division devised a method of assault based on the coordinated action of a tank company and an infantry company (see figure 5). Units attacked on a front usually three fields wide and always assaulted the center field last. The attack began as engineer teams or dozer tanks gapped the first hedgerow and indirect fire fell on and behind the forward German positions. An entire tank platoon then attacked with one section moving forward along each hedgerow paralleling the axis of advance. The Shermans put main-gun fire into the hedgerow to their front and sprayed the side hedgerows with heavy machine-gun fire. During the early phase of the assault, the tanks moved slowly enough so that supporting infantry could move with them and provide local security. The tanks also tried to protect themselves against German close infantry assaults by always staying at least twenty yards away from the nearest hedgerow. After reaching the main German defensive position, the tanks turned inward and worked their way toward the center of the field, covering the hedgerows with heavy machine-gun fire. Together, the tanks and infantry cleared the German defensive position and then prepared to continue the attack.[63]

The second phase of the assault began when engineers or dozer tanks gapped the hedgerows bordering the center field. Assault teams of infantry and tanks from each of the original attacking platoons then attacked the flanks of the center German position. During the second phase of the attack, follow-on forces moved forward to occupy the hedgerow delineating the original line of departure and provided suppressive fire with tank cannon and machine guns. The attacking sections moved toward the center of the German position, spraying the hedgerow with machine-gun fire and rooting out any remaining defenders. Once the final objective was secure, the companies reorganized and prepared to continue the attack by repeating the same sequence of events.[64]

The 3d Armored Division's hedgerow tactics had several merits. By not directly attacking each field with frontal assaults, the tankers hoped to secure a maximum amount of terrain while minimizing exposure to enemy fire. Commanders believed that by initially attacking and securing the outside fields that the Germans defending the center would withdraw to maintain the overall continuity of the German defense.[65]

On 29 June, Combat Command A (CCA) of 3d Armored Division entered battle in support of the 29th Infantry Division. General Hickey's mission was to reduce a German salient that protruded into the American lines near the hamlet of Villiers-

Phase I

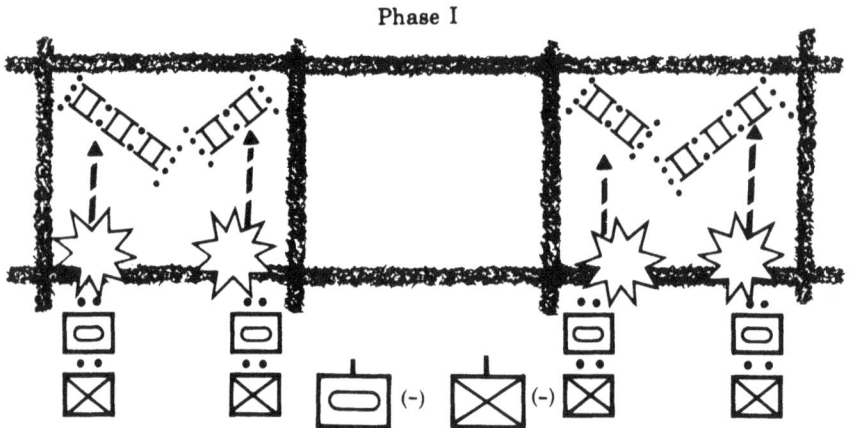

Phase I—Dozer tanks or engineer teams gap hedgerows as indirect fire falls on German positions. Tank and infantry teams attack along outer edges of fields, then sweep across the objective.

Phase II

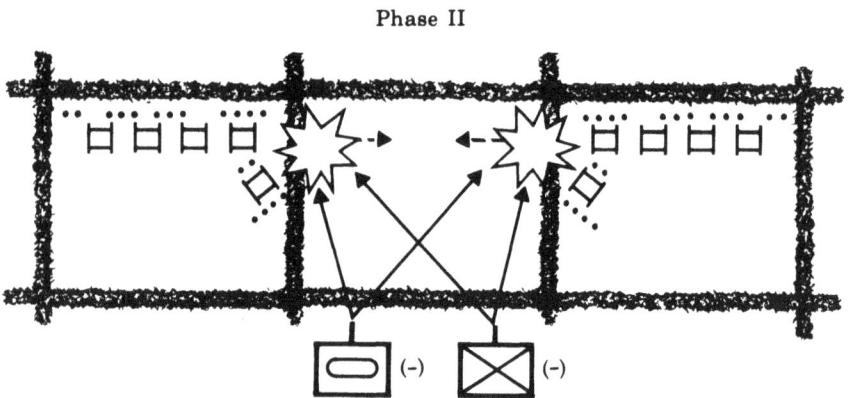

Phase II—Parent companies move forward and provide suppressive fire as friendly forces gap hedgerows of center field. Tank and infantry teams assault German position from the flanks.

LEGEND

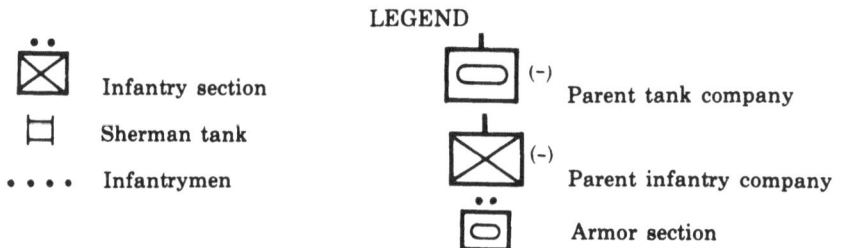

Infantry section

Sherman tank

• • • • Infantrymen

Parent tank company (-)

Parent infantry company (-)

Armor section

Figure 5. The 3d Armored Division's hedgerow tactics

A U.S. infantry squad deployed along a small hedgerow

Fossard. The position was heavily defended and at its furthest point jutted 2,000 yards into American lines. The XIX Corps ordered CCA to conduct a forward passage of lines through the 29th Division, attack and reduce the salient, and then defend until relieved by follow-on units of the 29th Division.[66]

CCA's attack against Villiers-Fossard moved forward at 0900 on 29 June after a punishing fifty-minute preparatory bombardment by fighter-bombers of the IX Tactical Air Command and seventeen battalions of artillery. The attacking battalions initially met fierce resistance, but coordinated tank-infantry-engineer teams successfully pushed the Germans back. The command's twelve dozer tanks played a major role in breaching the hedgerows. By the evening of 30 June, CCA successfully reduced the German salient and was relieved by the 29th Division.[67]

CCA's attack proved that coordinated combined arms actions could overcome the German hedgerow defense, but it also revealed the Germans were a determined and resourceful enemy. During the attack, the lead American infantry elements noticed that extensive wire communications ran between all German positions. The communications network enabled forward observers in trees to bring down accurate mortar and artillery fire on CCA. In the two-day attack, German indirect fire caused 351 out of the total of 401 American casualties. Not one Sherman was lost while moving through the hedgerows with infantry protection. However, an uncoordinated armor assault in the last phase of the operation again showed the necessity for combined arms action. In an unsupported blitz attack across the open spaces of an abandoned airfield south of Villiers-Fossard, elements of CCA lost twenty-seven Shermans. Long-range antitank fires hit thirteen tanks, while German *panzerfausts* destroyed another fourteen Shermans. Even with the loss of 27 of its 116 tanks, the use of effective combined arms tactics permitted CCA to reduce the Villiers-Fossard salient with a relatively low cost in men and equipment.[68]

The 2d Armored Division also developed special tactics for use in the hedgerows, but its techniques differed radically from those developed by other divisions within First Army. In mid-July, 2d Armored Division began to prepare for its role in Operation Cobra, First Army's offensive designed to rupture the defenses of the German Seventh Army and precipitate a major breakout into the Brittany peninsula and the interior of France. In the Cobra plan, First Army assigned a rapid exploitation mission to Major General Edward H. Brooks of the 2d Armored Division. The tactical challenge facing the 2d Armored was to develop techniques that allowed infantry and armor to work closely together during high-speed maneuvers through the Bocage.

By 25 July, CCA of the 2d Armored and the 22d Infantry had developed a novel way for tanks and infantry to cooperate during fast-moving operations: the infantry rode on the back decks of tanks and only dismounted when the attack met stiff enemy resistance. The overall tactical plan developed by Brigadier General Maurice A. Rose's CCA and the 22d Infantry called for units to attack in three assault waves. The first echelon consisted solely of tanks and relied on its own mobility and firepower, along with supporting artillery, to eliminate enemy positions. A second wave of tanks and infantry closely followed the lead elements. Eight infantrymen rode on the back deck of each Sherman in the second wave. The infantry had two main purposes. They provided tanks in the second wave with local security, and whenever the tanks in the first wave encountered stiff resistance, the infantry dismounted and worked

Infantrymen ride on the back of an M-4 Sherman "rhino" tank as it bashes through a hedgerow

with the lead tanks to conduct a coordinated combined arms attack. The third echelon also consisted of tanks and infantry and had the mission of eliminating positions bypassed or not detected by the leading elements.[69]

Between 19—25 July, the 22d Infantry and CCA's 66th Armored Regiment conducted mock attacks and rehearsals in preparation for Cobra. Tankers conducted classes on the proper

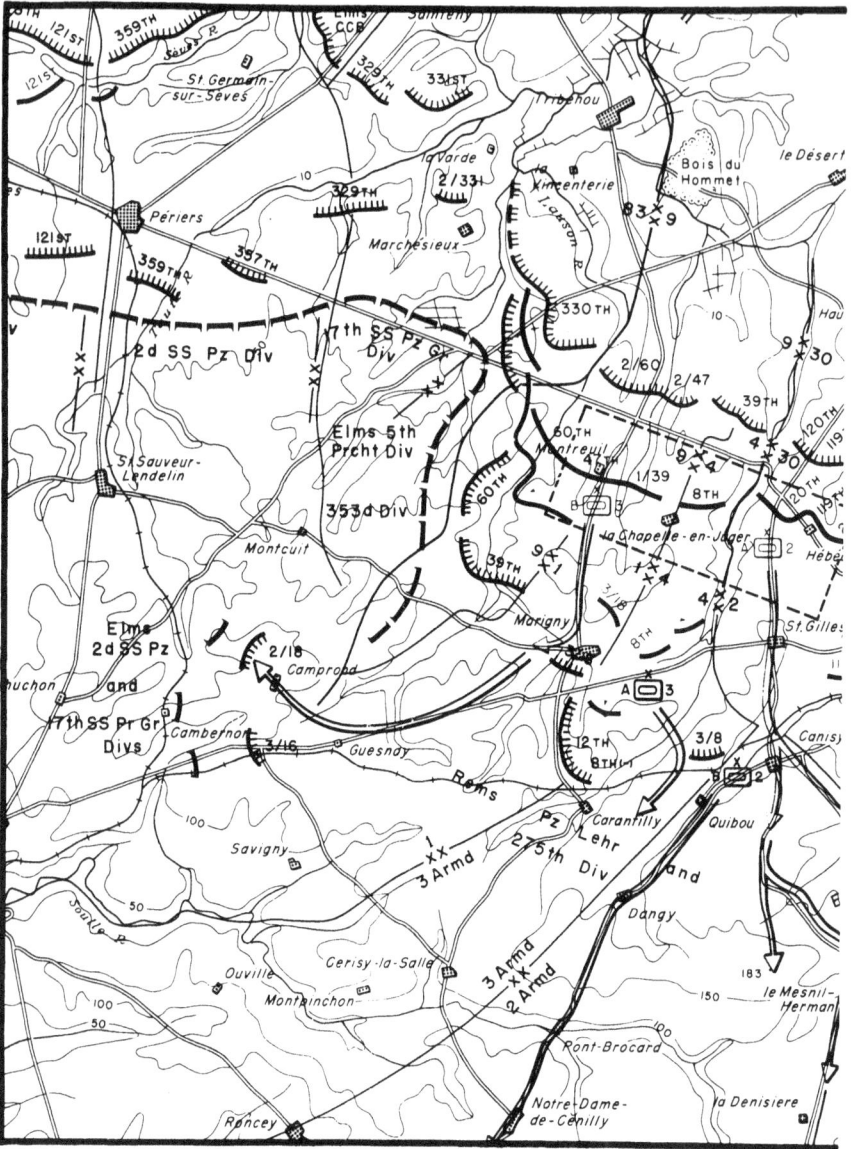

Map 4. Breakthrough, 25—27 July 1944

distribution of main-gun and machine-gun fire and the correct way to use the "rhinoceros" hedge cutters mounted on 75 percent of the 66th's tanks. Platoons from the 22d Infantry constantly practiced tank-infantry coordination with the 66th Armored.

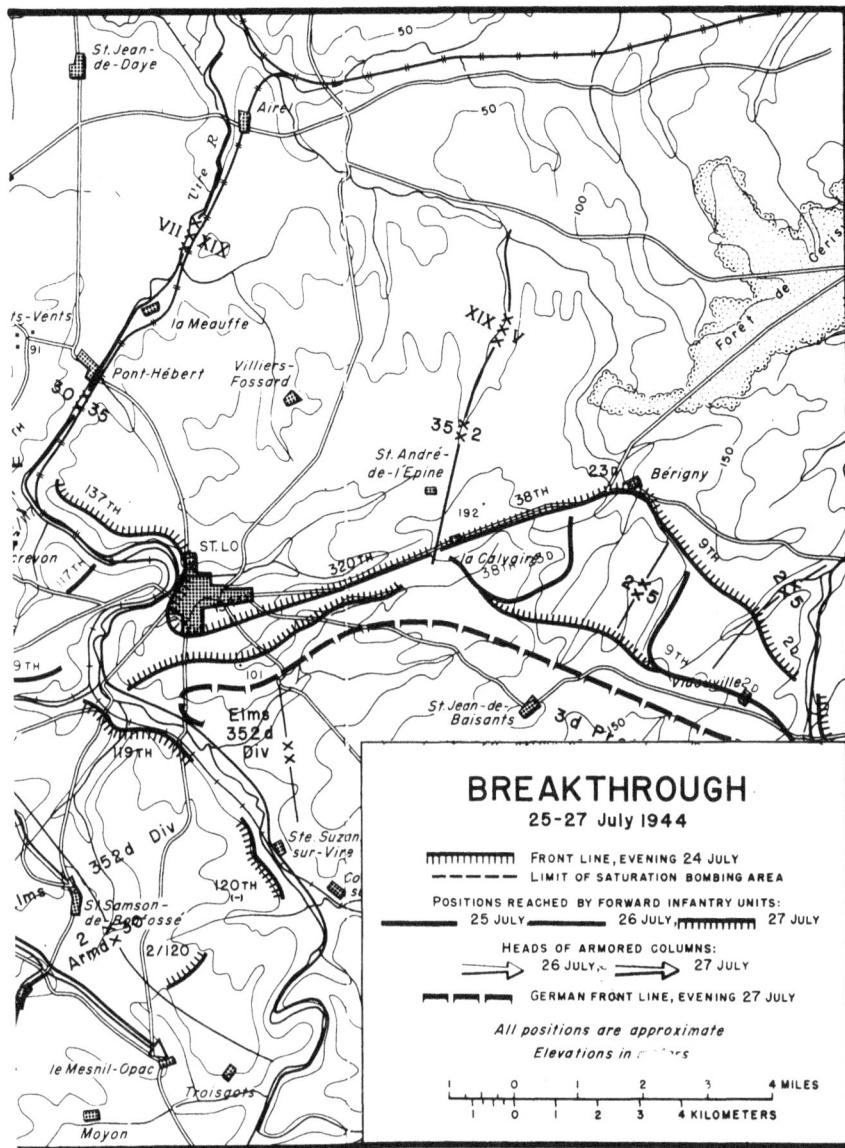

BREAKTHROUGH

25-27 July 1944

FRONT LINE, EVENING 24 JULY
LIMIT OF SATURATION BOMBING AREA

POSITIONS REACHED BY FORWARD INFANTRY UNITS:
25 JULY   26 JULY,   27 JULY

HEADS OF ARMORED COLUMNS:
26 JULY   27 JULY

GERMAN FRONT LINE, EVENING 27 JULY

All positions are approximate
Elevations in meters

4 MILES

4 KILOMETERS

(Source: From *Breakout and Pursuit* [Washington, D.C.: U.S. Army, Office of the Chief of Military History, 1961; reprint ed., Washington, D.C.: U.S. Army, Office of the Chief of Military History, 1978], map V.)

Infantry units learned how best to mount, dismount, and ride on tanks and taught their soldiers how to use the new external telephones mounted on most of CCA's tanks. Infantrymen also found ways to camouflage themselves with vegetation while riding on Shermans. Leaders generally found that infantrymen easily adapted to the new tasks involved in working with armor.[70]

On the morning of 26 July, the day after the saturation bombing that marked the opening of the Cobra offensive, CCA, applying some of its new techniques, conducted a forward passage of lines through the 30th Infantry Division and attacked southward (see map 4). General Rose's mission was to seize high ground in the vicinity of Hill 193 and le Mesnil-Herman and then establish defensive positions to repel German counter-attacks aimed at American follow-on forces. CCA's attack was the type of action most preferred by American commanders, a highly fluid situation in which mobile forces overran or by-passed enemy resistance.[71]

As a result of their new tactics and the intensive prebattle training period, CCA and the 22d Infantry made spectacular gains during the attack. The combined arms team worked closely together. Artillery observers rode in the lead tanks and brought accurate, indirect fire down on the enemy. Infantry battalion commanders with manpack radios rode in command tanks to better coordinate tankers and riflemen. The commander of the 22d Infantry reported that his soldiers were enthusiastic about riding the Shermans "Russian style." The infantry found that riding on tanks gave them several advantages. The height of the tanks put the riflemen above grazing fire and gave them better observation. Riding on tanks that moved at irregular speeds also made the infantry more difficult targets. In two days, CCA penetrated more than six miles into the German Seventh Army's sector. Cobra's preparatory bombardment, sporadic German resistance, and the coordination and swift execution of CCA's attack resulted in light casualties for the Americans. By nightfall of 27 July, General Rose was on his objective, having lost only 3 tanks and less than 200 men.[72]

For First Army, 6 June—31 July was a period of great adapt-ability, as unit commanders and their soldiers came to grips with the problems of fighting in the hedgerow country. For the most part, solutions to the problems confronting American units were both technical and tactical in nature. The greatest changes took place in combat units where tankers, infantrymen, engi-neers, and artillery forward observers became close-knit partners in a coordinated effort to root the Germans out of their defensive positions. With the opening of the Cobra offensive on 25 July,

First Army began to leave the Bocage behind and to impose on the German Army a new war of mobility and firepower.

———————————

III. CONCLUSIONS

The U.S. Army's first major fight in the European Theater of Operations in World War II was one of its hardest. Not until the Huertgen Forest or the German Ardennes offensive would American units be so challenged in battle. In Normandy, First Army gained institutional experience concerning how to conduct large-scale maneuvers, and inexperienced troops became either casualties or seasoned veterans. The fighting produced several operational and tactical lessons. Some were obvious to the participants at the time, others were lost or became blurred by the turbulence of battle.

Even when First Army failed to seize terrain and make large advances during the fighting in the hedgerows, it achieved, in considerable degree, the principal objective of combat operations: the destruction of enemy forces. The terrible carnage of the hedgerow fighting cannot help but impress anyone studying the Normandy campaign. By 17 July, the Germans had suffered almost 100,000 casualties but were unable to replace many of their losses. Only enough fresh troops arrived in Normandy to replace 12 percent of the losses. First Army had fared little better but was capable of replacing more of its casualties. Before D-Day, SHAEF planners expected over 70 percent casualties among infantrymen. By 31 July, First Army had suffered 100,000 casualties and 85 percent of these were among infantry units. The 29th Infantry Division alone, which was in continuous combat longer than any other division in First Army, suffered 9,939 casualties. Rifle companies throughout the U.S. Army often numbered about 100 men—or less than half strength. By the middle of July, infantry losses were so serious that First Army put in an immediate request for an additional 25,000 infantry replacements.[1]

In the Normandy campaign, the U.S. Army demonstrated its capability to adapt to a new and hostile environment. Confronting an experienced enemy in the Bocage—terrain that distinctly favored the defender—First Army devised tactics and combat procedures to meet unanticipated challenges. Furthermore, American troops showed a remarkable capacity to learn from their mistakes and experiences. Leaders learned in combat how best to use their organic weapons and equipment. At the small-unit level, junior officers, sergeants, and enlisted men invented ways to solve tactical problems peculiar to close combat in the hedgerows.

Not only did the Army adapt, but it did so quickly and in a great number of ways. The U.S. forces that crossed the Normandy beaches in June had changed a great deal by late July. Between D-Day and the Normandy breakout, First Army had devised numerous technical and tactical solutions for the conduct of battles against the German Army. The greatest transformation took place in combat units where tankers, infantrymen, engineers, and artillery forward observers became close-knit partners in a coordinated effort. In the preinvasion period, tankers probably could not have visualized the hedge cutters and back-deck telephones that were to be on most of their tanks by the opening of the Cobra offensive. Nor could commanders have imagined the tactical combinations that had to be developed for combat in the Bocage. By the end of July, First Army routinely used a large number of combat techniques and procedures that were unheard of in the preinvasion period.

Ideas on how to achieve better results against the Germans came from a wide variety of sources. In general, ideas flowed upward from the men actually engaged in battle and were then either approved or rejected by higher commanders. Within the bottom ranks of the Army, individual soldiers suggested ways that enabled their units to move against the enemy. Sergeant Culin's hedgerow cutter is the best example of a single soldier's idea that influenced all of First Army. At the top end of the chain of command, general officers also produced ideas on how to defeat the Germans. General Cota's supervision of the development of hedgerow tactics in the 29th Division typifies the contributions made by general officers.

The effort to gather ideas on how to beat the Germans was decentralized. There was almost no effort to work out an Army-wide solution to the tactical problems of combat in the Bocage. The First Army staff made no distinct attempt to devise tactical solutions for the whole command to use in overcoming the German defenses. First Army did publish and distribute to all units a series of "Battle Experiences," reports that contained information and lessons learned in battle. The bulletins were not directive in nature, but subordinate commanders were expected to use the information to assist them in finding ways to defeat the Germans. In fact, in only one area did First Army headquarters take an active role in dealing with tactical problems: the production and distribution of Sergeant Culin's hedgerow cutter.

What explains the decentralized, collective method of tactical problem solving exhibited within First Army? First, the U.S. Army was not in a position to analyze the German defense systematically and produce one *best* solution for attacking through the hedgerows. First Army simply did not have the time to slow the pace of combat operations while seeking a uniform, coordinated solution to tactical problems. The U.S. Army had to push inland and expand its beachhead as a prelude to larger operations. Corps and division commanders received orders and were expected to execute them as quickly as possible while overcoming all difficulties. Commanders who did not perform well were relieved; several division commanders lost their posts during the Normandy campaign.

Combat in the hedgerows emphasized the need for competent, assertive leadership in commanders at all levels. Army doctrine insisted that the coordination of the tactics and techniques of the combined arms team was a command function. In Normandy, commanders were held responsible for developing and implementing solutions to tactical problems and were often given wide latitude in finding answers to difficulties. Senior American leaders expected their subordinate commanders to develop and execute solutions to overcome obstacles instead of waiting for staffs from higher headquarters to devise the most workable answers to tactical problems. Commanders within each division listened to ideas from their units, learned from the experiences of other divisions, and then developed their own tactics for overcoming the German hedgerow defenses. While commanders throughout First Army developed new tactical methods that capitalized on the firepower and mobility of the combined arms team, the tactics used within each division were somewhat different. The variations in technique reflected the individual ideas and experiences of commanders at all levels within each division concerning how to best attack through the hedgerows.

The newly developed tactical methods played a significant role in the defeat of the Germans. Though perhaps not in themselves decisive, new tactical and technical innovations allowed American units to move forward against the Germans while suffering significantly fewer casualties. The attacks against the Villiers-Fossard salient, the Martinville ridge, and Hill 192 by the 3d Armored, 29th, and 2d Infantry Divisions, respectively, are the best examples of combined arms attacks that made good progress with few casualties. Without the development and use of special hedgerow tactics, the U.S. Army might have become bogged down in a brutal war of attrition with the Germans—a situation that would have morally and materially disrupted the Allied war effort.

The Normandy campaign illustrates the importance of pre-combat training in preparing soldiers for battle. Serious training deficiencies led to ineffective cooperation between the combat arms in the early hedgerow fighting. A First Army report warned that the "development of operational procedures and techniques between the infantry and close-support tanks must not be left until arrival in the combat zone."[2] Yet this is exactly what happened. Standard tank-infantry training was poor in the Army. Surprisingly, after two years of actual combat in other theaters, the U.S. Army still placed too little emphasis on the thorough training of tank-infantry teams. Moreover, the lack of an organic tank battalion within each infantry division prevented armor and infantry units from training together on a regular basis. Training weaknesses also existed in each of the combat arms. Infantrymen lacked aggressiveness and failed to use their organic weapons. Tankers initially showed a great reluctance to leave roads and thus avoid enemy antitank fire. Combined arms teams did demonstrate effective coordination between infantry and artillery units—a bright spot in their record. While inadequate training hampers any unit in combat, the peculiar nature of the Bocage particularly magnified the effects of training weaknesses among the combat arms.

Deprived of combined arms training opportunities prior to D-Day, combat training conducted just behind the front lines played a key role in the success of American operations. During such training, tankers and infantrymen familiarized themselves with each other's capabilities and methods and conducted remedial training on how to work together under fire. Finding technical and tactical solutions to overcome the German defenses would not ensure success; soldiers still had to be trained and drilled on how to use new mechanical devices and execute novel hedgerow tactics. Training conducted in rear areas by the 29th, 2d, and 83d Infantry Divisions and the 2d and 3d Armored Divisions typified the combat zone training experiences that took place throughout First Army.

One of the U.S. Army's greatest shortcomings in the campaign was its ignorance of the characteristics of the Bocage. Prior to D-Day, senior leaders had no proper appreciation of the hostile nature of the hedgerow country. Despite accurate, detailed analyses by SHAEF and First Army staffs about the military characteristics of the hedgerow country, commands at the highest level did nothing to prepare for combat in the hedgerows. Even though U.S. forces were properly concerned about preparing for the amphibious landings, they failed to see beyond the beaches and to plan and prepare for the battle in the Normandy countryside. With some training, units might have been more prepared for combat in the hedgerows.

The American tendency to rely on the lavish use of firepower is another striking feature of First Army's conduct of the Normandy campaign. To expend munitions rather than human lives is certainly a sound practice, but combat in the Bocage proved that firepower alone cannot defeat the enemy. Despite awesome preparatory bombardments, the Germans still stood and fought and had to be killed or captured by American infantrymen and tankers. An important battlefield lesson of the Normandy campaign is that aggressive tactical maneuver must be combined with the proper use of offensive fires in order to defeat a well-prepared defender.

A study of combat in the hedgerows also sheds some light on the fighting abilities of the opposing forces. Several recent works in military history have analyzed the relative combat performance of German and American units in World War II. In general, these studies argue that the German Army is the paradigm of operational and tactical success, while the American Army muddles through to victory by the application of overwhelming resources and thundering firepower. In *Fighting Power*, Martin van Creveld argues that the U.S. Army put more emphasis on technical and administrative matters than on the psychological needs of the fighting soldier and the training of small-unit leaders. Knowledgeable employment of weapons and machines did play a key role in the American victory, but not to the extent where other considerations were disregarded. Max Hastings, in *Overlord*, praises German fighting ability while criticizing the U.S. Army for weaknesses in its combat performance. However, Hastings fails to extend his analysis and does not examine how First Army did overcome problems in the Bocage. Even a classic work like S. L. A. Marshall's *Men Against Fire* does not give a complete picture of the fighting in the hedgerows. Marshall observed that in Normandy only 15 to 25 percent of infantry soldiers fired their weapons in combat. While such a low fire ratio may be correct, Marshall does not adequately explain why the volume of small-arms fire was so meager nor how the U.S. Army overcame prepared German defenses despite alleged deficiencies in American infantry units. Undoubtedly, First Army experienced problems in its combat units, but this study attempts to portray a more complete and even-handed appraisal of American fighting prowess than that depicted in recent analyses of American soldiers' combat performance. While the U.S. Army contained a number of officers and soldiers who proved weak and incompetent in combat, many others displayed the ability to perform under pressure, to get maximum results from available resources, and to lead their comrades in battle.

More than anything else, the Normandy campaign is an excellent example of how a military organization can adapt itself to unforeseen circumstances and a hostile environment. American operations in the Bocage prove that Michael Howard's assertion is largely correct: a successful army must have the ability to change and adapt under fire in order to develop correct methods for overcoming the enemy. In this respect, First Army performed well in Normandy and laid the foundation for operations that eventually carried U.S. armies beyond the Rhine and to victory.

NOTES

Chapter 1

1. Michael Howard, "Military Science in an Age of Peace," *Journal of the Royal United Services Institute for Defence Studies,* 119 (March 1974):3—9.

2. Russell Frank Weigley, *Eisenhower's Lieutenants: The Campaign of France and Germany, 1944—1945* (Bloomington: Indiana University Press, 1981), 22—23.

3. Ibid., 24.

4. Ibid., 14—19.

5. Ibid., 23; and U.S. War Department, Field Manual 100-5, *Field Service Regulations: Operations* (Washington, DC: U.S. Government Printing Office, 1941), 278—80.

6. U.S. War Department, Field Manual 17-36, *Employment of Tanks with Infantry* (Washington, DC: U.S. Government Printing Office, 1944), 3—10.

7. FM 100-5, ii—19.

8. Ibid.

9. Ibid., 97—103, 109—19.

10. U.S. War Department, Field Manual 7-20, *Rifle Battalion* (Washington, DC: U.S. Government Printing Office, 1942), 80—87.

11. FM 100-5, 5.

12. FM 17-36, 1.

13. Ibid., 25—65.

14. U.S. War Department, Field Manual 6-20, *Field Artillery Tactics and Technique* (Washington, DC: U.S. Government Printing Office, 1940), 97—103, 128—31.

15. FM 100-5, 14—15.

16. Weigley, *Eisenhower's Lieutenants*, 24—28; and Major General Ernest N. Harmon, U.S. Army, "Notes on Combat Experience During the Tunisian and African Campaigns," n.d., 15—17, available at the manuscript collection, U.S. Army Armor School Library, Fort Knox, Kentucky.

17. Harmon, "Notes," 3.

18. Ibid., 6—9.

19. Ibid., 11—13.

20. Martin Blumenson, *Breakout and Pursuit,* U.S. Army in World War II (Washington, DC: Office of the Chief of Military History, Department of the Army, 1961), chaps. 1—3 passim. All factual material in this section is from the cited reference unless otherwise noted.

21. Ibid., 178.

22. Omar Nelson Bradley and Clay Blair, *A General's Life* (New York: Simon and Schuster, 1983), 247—59.

23. Ibid., 262—64.

24. Ibid., 266—71.

Chapter 2

1. "Appreciation on Possible Development of Operations to Secure a Lodgment Area: Operation OVERLORD," a terrain analysis study of the Cotentin Peninsula, 3 May 1942, 7, Brigadier General Arthur S. Nevins, U.S. Army, Papers, U.S. Army Military History Institute, Carlisle Barracks, Pennsylvania; and Blumenson, *Breakout and Pursuit*, 177. The U.S. Army Military History Institute is hereafter cited as USAMHI.

2. "Operations to Secure a Lodgment Area," Nevins Papers, 5; Lieutenant Colonel Chester B. Hansen, U.S. Army, Diaries, 8—9 June 1944, USAMHI; and James Maurice Gavin, *On to Berlin: Battles of an Airborne Commander, 1943—1946* (New York: Viking Press, 1978), 121.

3. Captain Charles D. Folsom, U.S. Army, "Hedgerow Fighting Near Carentan," Army School Library Report 41-53 (Advanced Officers' Class no. 1, U.S. Army Armor School, Fort Knox, Kentucky, 1948), 1; and U.S. Army Ground Forces Observer Board, European Theater of Operations, *Reports of the Army Ground Forces Board, European Theater of Operations*, Report no. 171, "Normandy Hedgerows," 1—2, hereafter cited as AGF Obs. Bd., ETO, Rept. no. and the individual report title. There were AGF Observer Boards for each World War II theater of operations, and at one point observers were operating for both the War Department and the AGF and filed their reports under the aegis of the War Department while intending them for the AGF. The six-volume collection at USAMHI contains reports bearing both headings but is considered representative of AGF reports.

4. Blumenson, *Breakout and Pursuit*, 48—50.

5. AGF Obs. Bd., ETO, Rept. no. 138, "Notes on Hedgerow Warfare in the Normandy Beachhead," 1—2; AGF Obs. Bd., ETO, Rept. no. 141, "German Defense in Hedgerow Terrain," Exhibit A; AGF Obs. Bd., ETO, Rept. no. 195, "Lessons from Present Campaign," 1—4; U.S. Army, XIX Corps, "The Tank-Infantry Team," 24 June 1944, 2—3, available at USAMHI; and U.S. Army, 1st U.S. Army Group, "Battle Experiences," no. 1, 1, available at USAMHI, hereafter cited as FUSAG, "Battle Experiences." During the Normandy fighting, 1st Army Group published and distributed a series of "Battle Experiences," reports that contained technical information and a synopsis of key lessons learned in combat by subordinate units.

6. Ibid.; FUSAG, "Battle Experiences," no. 1, 3; and FUSAG, "Battle Experiences," no. 12, 2.

7. FUSAG, "Battle Experiences," no. 1, 2; AGF Obs. Bd., ETO, Rept. no. 195, 1—4; and U.S. Army, 1st Army, *First United States Army: Report of Operations, 20 October 1943—1 August 1944*, 14 vols. (Washington, DC: U.S. War Department, 1945?), 1:122—23, hereafter cited as "First Army Report."

8. Ibid.

9. Ibid.

10. First Army Report, 1:117; AGF Obs. Bd., ETO, Rept. no. 157, "Notes on Interviews with Various Infantry Commanders in Normandy," 1; and FUSAG, "Battle Experiences," no. 14, 1—2.

11. AGF Obs. Bd., ETO, Rept. no. 187, "Training Memoranda, VII U.S. Army Corps," Exhibit B, 1.

12. First Army Report, 1:117; FUSAG, "Battle Experiences," no. 1, 3; and FUSAG, "Battle Experiences," no. 14, 1—2.

13. FUSAG, "Battle Experiences," no. 10, 1.

14. Ibid., no. 19, 1.

15. AGF, Obs. Bd., ETO, Rept. no. 157, 1, 4, 10.

16. Major William R. Campbell, U.S. Army, "Tanks with Infantry," Armor School Library Report 42-9 (Advanced Officers' Class no. 1, U.S. Army Armor School, Fort Knox, Kentucky, 1947), 1.

17. First Army Report, 1:121—22; and AGF Obs. Bd., ETO, Rept. no. 157, 5.

18. First Army Report, 1:121; and AGF Obs. Bd., ETO, Rept. no. 187, Exhibit B, 1.

19. Omar Nelson Bradley, A Soldier's Story (1951; reprint, New York: Rand McNally, 1978), 306—7; and Blumenson, Breakout and Pursuit, 42—43.

20. First Army Report, 1:122; and AGF Obs. Bd., ETO, Rept. no. 195, 1—3.

21. Hansen, Diaries, 9 June 1944.

22. First Army Report, 1:122; and AGF Obs. Bd., ETO, Rept. no. 195, 1—3.

23. AGF Obs. Bd., ETO, Rept. no. 201, "Use of Dozer Tanks and Landing of Tanks in Amphibious Operations," 1.

24. U.S. Forces, European Theater, Reports of the General Board, Study no. 52, "Armored Special Equipment," 14—17, available at USAMHI, hereafter cited as USFET, Reports.

25. AGF Obs. Bd., ETO, Rept. no. 191, "Notes on Interviews with Various Commanders in Normandy," 2—3, and Exhibits A, B, and C.

26. Ibid.

27. Ibid.

28. Ibid.

29. Ibid.

30. Ibid.

31. Folsom, "Hedgerow Fighting," 5; AGF Obs. Bd., ETO, Rept. no. 191, 5; and Blumenson, Breakout and Pursuit, 206.

32. Max Hastings, Overlord: D-Day and the Battle for Normandy (London: Michael Joseph, 1984), 252; and Blumenson, Breakout and Pursuit, 206—7.

33. Major William C. Sylvan, U.S. Army, Diaries, 14 July 1944, USAMHI; and Bradley, *A Soldier's Story*, 342.

34. Ibid.; and First Army Report, 5:200—201.

35. James J. Butler, "Individual Tank-Infantry Communications," *Armored Cavalry Journal* 56 (July-August 1947):43—45; FM 17-36, 93—100; and Blumenson, *Breakout and Pursuit*, 43.

36. Butler, "Communications," 43—45; and First Army Report, 1:122.

37. Folsom, "Hedgerow Fighting," 7; and AGF Obs. Bd., ETO, Rept. no. 120, "Employment of Tanks with Infantry," 4—5.

38. Butler, "Communications," 44—45; AGF Obs. Bd., ETO, Rept. no. 120, 4—5; and FUSAG, "Battle Experiences," no. 13, 12.

39. USFET, *Reports*, Study no. 50, "Organization, Equipment, and Tactical Employment of Separate Tank Battalions," 6—7.

40. AGF Obs. Bd., ETO, Rept. no. Misc.-19, "Information Regarding Air-Ground Joint Operations," 8; and U.S. Army, G-3 Staff, Historical Branch, Programs Division, "Historical Survey of Army Fire Support" (Washington, DC, 1963), I-B-2, loaned to the author by Dr. Allan R. Millett.

41. AGF Obs. Bd., ETO, Rept. no. Misc.-19, 8; First Army Report, 1:123; and AGF Obs. Bd., ETO, Rept. no. 192, "Corps Artillery," 5.

42. Gordon A. Harrison, *Cross-Channel Attack*, United States Army in World War II (Washington, DC: Office of the Chief of Military History, U.S. Army, 1950), 381—84.

43. Ibid.

44. Major Forrest W. Creamer, U.S. Army, "Operations of the XIX U.S. Army Corps in Normandy," Armor School Library Report 42-8 (Advanced Officers' Class no. 1, U.S. Army Armor School, Fort Knox, Kentucky, 1947), 31; and AGF Obs. Bd., ETO, Rept. no. 191, Exhibit A.

45. AGF Obs. Bd., ETO, Rept. no. 138, Exhibit A.

46. Ibid.

47. Ibid.

48. AGF Obs. Bd., ETO, Rept. no. 157, 2.

49. Blumenson, *Breakout and Pursuit*, 153—57; and U.S. War Department, General Staff, *St. Lo, 7 July—19 July 1944*, American Forces in Action Series (1947; reprint, Washington, DC: U.S. Army Center of Military History, 1984), 54—58, hereafter cited as WDGS, *St. Lo*.

50. Ibid.

51. Ibid.; and AGF Obs. Bd., ETO, Rept. no. 191, 1.

52. Blumenson, *Breakout and Pursuit*, 149—53; and WDGS, *St. Lo*, 58—69.

53. FUSAG, "Battle Experiences," no. 8, 1—2.

54. Blumenson, *Breakout and Pursuit*, 149—53; and WDGS, *St. Lo*, 58—69.

55. Ibid.

56. Ibid.; and FUSAG, "Battle Experiences," no. 8, 2.

57. Folsom, "Hedgerow Fighting," 1—10.

58. Ibid.

59. Ibid.

60. Blumenson, *Breakout and Pursuit*, 78—86.

61. Creamer, "Operations," 18—22.

62. Ibid.

63. AGF Obs. Bd., ETO, Rept. no. 141, Exhibit A.

64. Ibid.

65. Ibid.

66. Creamer, "Operations," 20—28.

67. Ibid.

68. Ibid.

69. AGF Obs. Bd., ETO, Rept. no. 191, 6—7.

70. Ibid.; and Advanced Officers' Class no. 1, Committee 3, "Employment of 2d Armored Division in Operation COBRA," Armor School Library Report 45.2-3 (U.S. Army Armor School, Fort Knox, Kentucky, 1950), 8—16.

71. Blumenson, *Breakout and Pursuit*, 254—57.

72. Ibid.; and AGF Obs. Bd., ETO, Rept. no. 191, 6—7.

Chapter 3

1. Hastings, *Overlord*, 210; AGF Obs. Bd., ETO, Rept. no. 191, 2; and Blumenson, *Breakout and Pursuit*, 175—79.

2. First Army Report, 1:117.

BIBLIOGRAPHY

PRIMARY SOURCES

Personal Papers and Interviews

Hansen, Chester B., Lieutenant Colonel, U.S. Army. Diaries, U.S. Army Military History Institute, Carlisle Barracks, Pennsylvania. Lieutenant Colonel Hansen served as General Bradley's personal aide throughout World War II.

Nevins, Arthur S., Brigadier General, U.S. Army. Papers. U.S. Army Military History Institute, Carlisle Barracks, Pennsylvania. Brigadier General Nevins served on the SHAEF staff as assistant operations officer throughout World War II and was intimately involved in the planning for Operation Overlord.

Sylvan, William C., Major, U.S. Army. Diaries. U.S. Army Military History Institute, Carlisle Barracks, Pennsylvania. Major Sylvan served as General Courtney H. Hodges' aide throughout World War II.

Reports

Campbell, William R., Major, U.S. Army, "Tanks with Infantry." Advanced Officers' Class no. 1, U.S. Army Armor School, Fort Knox, Kentucky, 1947. Armor School Library Report 42-9. Major Campbell served with the 1st Infantry Division during the Normandy campaign.

Creamer, Forrest W., Major, U.S. Army, "Operations of the XIX U.S. Army Corps in Normandy." Advanced Officers' Class no. 1, U.S. Army Armor School, Fort Knox, Kentucky, 1947. Armor School Library Report 42-8. Major Creamer served as assistant operations officer on the XIX Corps staff during the Normandy campaign.

Folsom, Charles D., Captain, U.S. Army. "Hedgerow Fighting Near Carentan." Advanced Officers' Class no. 1, U.S. Army Armor School, Fort Knox, Kentucky, 1948. Armor School Library Report 41-53. Captain Folsom was a rifle company commander in the 329th Infantry, 83d Infantry Division, during the Normandy campaign.

Harmon, Ernest N., Major General, U.S. Army. "Notes on Combat Experience During the Tunisian and African Campaigns." N.d. Available at the manuscript collection, U.S. Army Armor School Library, Fort Knox, Kentucky.

U.S. Army. 1st Army. *Report of Operations, 20 October 1941—1 August 1944.* 14 vols. Washington, DC?: U.S. War Department, 1945?

U.S. Army. 1st Army Group. "Battle Experiences." 1944. Available at the U.S. Army Military History Institute, Carlisle Barracks, Pennsylvania.

U.S. Army Ground Forces Observer Board, European Theater of Operations. *Reports of the Army Ground Forces Observer Board, European Theater of Operations.* 6 vols. 1944—1945. Available at the U.S. Army Military History Institute, Carlisle Barracks, Pennsylvania.

U.S. Forces, European Theater. *Reports of the General Board.* 36 vols. November 1945. Available at the U.S. Army Military History Institute, Carlisle Barracks, Pennsylvania.

Books

Bradley, Omar Nelson. *A Soldier's Story.* 1951. Reprint. New York: Rand McNally, 1978.

Bradley, Omar Nelson, and Clay Blair. *A General's Life.* New York: Simon and Schuster, 1983.

Gavin, James Maurice. *On to Berlin: Battles of an Airborne Commander, 1943—1946.* New York: Viking Press, 1978.

SECONDARY SOURCES

Special Reports and Studies

Advanced Officers' Class no. 1, Committee 3. "Employment of 2d Armored Division in Operation COBRA." U.S. Army Armor School, Fort Knox, Kentucky, 1950.

Greenfield, Kent Roberts. *Army Ground Forces and the Air-Ground Battle Team Including Organic Light Aviation.* Study no. 35. Fort Monroe, VA: Historical Section, Army Ground Forces, 1948.

Ney, Virgil. *Evolution of the U.S. Army Division, 1939—1968.* Fort Belvoir, VA: Combat Operations Research Group, U.S. Army Combat Developments Command, 1969.

Tannler, Thomas K., et al. "A Critical Analysis of the History of Armor in World War II." Advanced Officers' Class no. 1, U.S. Army Armor School, Fort Knox, Kentucky, 1953.

U.S. Army. G-3 Staff. Historical Branch. Programs Division. "Historical Survey of Army Fire Support." Washington, DC, 1963. Loaned to the author by Dr. Allan R. Millett.

U.S. War Department. Field Manual 6-20. *Field Artillery Tactics and Technique.* Washington, DC: U.S. Government Printing Office, 1940.

——— . Field Manual 7-20. *Rifle Battalion.* Washington, DC: U.S. Government Printing Office, 1942.

——— . Field Manual 17-36. *Employment of Tanks with Infantry.* Washington, DC: U.S. Government Printing Office, 1944.

——— . Field Manual 100-5. *Field Service Regulations: Operations.* Washington, DC: U.S. Government Printing Office, 1941.

Books

Blumenson, Martin. *Breakout and Pursuit.* U.S. Army in World War II. Washington, DC: Office of the Chief of Military History, Department of the Army, 1961.

Harrison, Gordon A. *Cross-Channel Attack.* U.S. Army in World War II. Washington, DC: Office of the Chief of Military History, U.S. Army, 1950.

Hastings, Max. *Overlord: D-Day and the Battle for Normandy.* London: Michael Joseph, 1984.

Marshall, S. L. A. *Men Against Fire: The Problem of Battle Command in Future War.* 1947. Reprint. Gloucester, MA: Peter Smith, 1978.

U.S. Department of the Army, Historical Division. *Utah Beach to Cherbourg (6 June—27 June 1944).* American Forces in Action Series. 1948. Reprint. Washington, DC: U.S. Army Center of Military History, 1984.

U.S. War Department. General Staff. *St. Lo, 7 July—19 July 1944.* American Forces in Action Series. 1947. Reprint. Washington, DC: U.S. Army Center of Military History, 1984.

Van Creveld, Martin. *Fighting Power: German and U.S. Army Military Performance, 1914—1945.* London: Arms and Armour Press, 1983; Westport, CT: Greenwood Press, 1982.

Weigley, Russell Frank. *Eisenhower's Lieutenants: The Campaign of France and Germany, 1944—1945.* Bloomington: Indiana University Press, 1981.

Articles

Butler, James J. "Individual Tank-Infantry Communications." *Armored Cavalry Journal* 56 (July-August 1947):43—45.

Howard, Michael. "Military Science in an Age of Peace." *Journal of the Royal United Services Institute for Defence Studies* 119 (March 1974):3—9.

www.ingramcontent.com/pod-product-compliance
Lightning Source LLC
Chambersburg PA
CBHW070024110426
42741CB00034B/2469